W9-CDU-605

THE CENTERS OF CIVILIZATION SERIES

Damascus
UNDER THE
MAMLŪKS

Damascus

UNDER THE MAMLŪKS

•

by Nicola A. Ziadeh

•

UNIVERSITY OF OKLAHOMA PRESS

NORMAN

WINGATE COLLEGE LIBRARY
WINGATE, N. C.

Books in English by Nicola A. Ziadeh

Urban Life in Syria under the Early Mamlūks. Beirut, 1953.
Syria and Lebanon. New York and London, 1957.
Whither North Africa? Aligarh, 1957.
Sanūsīyah. Leiden, 1958.
Origins of Nationalism in Tunisia. Beirut, 1962.
Damascus Under the Mamlūks. Norman, 1964.

LIBRARY OF CONGRESS CATALOG CARD NUMBER: 64-11330

Copyright 1964 by the University of Oklahoma Press, Publishing Division of the University. Composed and printed at Norman, Oklahoma, U.S.A., by the University of Oklahoma Press.
First edition.

To my wife

46799

Preface

UNDER THE Mamlūks, Damascus enjoyed a variety of experiences which the present volume tries to place before the reader. Fortunately for me, a number of travelers interested themselves not only in visiting the city, but also in setting their impressions in writing. In this connection I wish to express my debt to the admirable English translation of Ibn Batuta by Sir Hamilton Gibb and R. J. C. Broadhurst's English translation of Ibn Jubayr, both of which were used extensively.

My thanks go to Miss Brenda Sens and Miss Carolyn Cross of the Center for Middle Eastern Studies, Harvard University, for their special care in typing the manuscript.

N. A. Z.

Beirut, Lebanon
January, 1964

Contents

	Preface	*page ix*
	Introduction	*xiii*
1.	The Mamlūks	3
2.	The Damascus of Saladin and Ibn Jubayr	23
3.	European Travelers in Damascus	34
4.	Damascus and Suburbs	48
5.	People and Problems	60
6.	City Administration	77
7.	Intellectual Life	92
	Bibliography	132
	Index	135

MAP

Damascus *xvii*

Introduction

Geography, history, and legend have made Damascus an eminent city. Situated at the edge of a plain, protected on the west and north by a mountain, and copiously endowed with water from the western slopes, Damascus commanded a position coveted by settlers from time immemorial. Man must have been attracted by this place which provided lands to be exploited, water to be used freely for irrigation and ablution, and a mountain for protection should enemies threaten. As communities grew and relations were established, Damascus became a pivotal center for its neighbors. From the dawn of history, people living to the south, east, or north of Damascus found themselves marching on the routes leading to it in order to secure needed commodities and to sell their produce. These commodities increased with the growth of civilization and the expansion of the area served, but Damascus always provided the needs. Its Ghūṭah, or garden, to the east produced vegetables and fruits of varied description; the areas a little farther removed provided the inhabitants and merchants with cereals; such raw materials

WINGATE COLLEGE LIBRARY
WINGATE, N. C.

as hides, bones, and, later, cotton came from regions not too far away. As trade relations developed, goods and merchandise of East and West were sold or exchanged in the marts of Damascus.

Routes connected the city with Aleppo in North Syria, and hence with Mesopotamia and Asia Minor; with Palmyra and later Baghdad, and from there to the countries of the Orient; south with Der'a, whence the routes continued to the Ḥijāz; with Palestine via the Lake of Tiberias, and hence with Egypt; and, last but not least, with Beirut and Sidon on the Lebanese coast, ports which connected the capital of the Aramaeans, the Ghassānids, the Umayyads, and modern Syria with the West.

You approach Damascus from the east, north, or south, on horse or by train, by car or plane, and immediately upon seeing it, with its Ghūṭah, you notice a change from the arid to the watered, from the desert to the sown, from the land of moving, scattered nomads to that of settled, confident communities. Nothing has demonstrated the pleasantness of Damascus to me more markedly than arriving there after an automobile trip from Jordan or Palmyra or a flight from Baghdad or Kuwait, especially in the dry season. You search in vain for a patch of grass, a tree, a bush, or a plant; when you come to Damascus, you have a view of deep-green orchards spreading in front of you.

Damascus claims to be the most ancient city in the world. Jericho has recently established its right to this claim, but Jericho is a small place compared to Damascus, and we are speaking of cities. This long history cannot be dealt with here, but neither can it be completely ignored.

This important location first drew the attention of the Aramaeans, who settled there sometime in the third millennium. As they became the masters of eastern land trade, Damascus developed with them and became a counterpart of Tyre and Sidon, marts of their cousins the Phoenicians. The center of the Aramaean city was the hilly part of ancient Damascus, not far from modern Ḥamīdīyah, where the temple and palace stood, with the markets and dwellings extended around them. Damascus was strong enough to lead a league of Syrian and Palestinian princes against the first Assyrian assaults, between the eleventh and eighth centuries B.C., but the Assyrians eventually came down like wolves, and all fell prey to them. Damascus, however, did not lose its importance as a pivot of trade routes, although from then on it was nothing more than a provincial capital, a position it held under the Assyrians, Chaldeans, Persians, Greeks, Romans, and Byzantines.

The Romans recognized the importance of Damascus more fully than their predecessors. They extended its area; it also became, indirectly, part of the Roman eastern limes. The wall that surrounded the city, and which continued to surround it for centuries, had an oblong form.

The Arab conquest of Damascus in 636 A.D. ushered a new era in the city's history. Not only were it and the surrounding area gradually transformed culturally, religiously, and linguistically, but between 661 and 750 it was the capital of an empire—the Umayyad Empire—which extended from the Indus to the Pyrenees. The caliphs must have built greatly there, as witness the Green Palace of Muʿāwiyah, the founder of the dynasty. But the one monument of the Umayyads which stands as a testimonial to their achievement is the Great Umayyad Mosque, around which centered the life of the Damascenes.

From the religious point of view, the transformation was not complete. Christians, tenaciously clinging to their faith, continued to live in the area, and although Antioch was at first the center of the diocese of the region, Damascus usurped that place, in the case of the Orthodox church, to which city the patriarchate was moved. In the Middle Ages, Christians, like Jews, had their own quarters.

The fall of the Umayyads in 750, and the rise of the 'Abbāsids, relegated Damascus to the backwaters of the empire. The city had tenacity, however, and its vitality assured it a respectable continuity, although not an ascendancy. Then came the Zangids, the Ayyūbids, and the Mamlūks, but more of this later.

* * *

How simple it is to give a historical account of a city! It is not so with legend. Legendary information is often so illogically intertwined that you cannot disentangle it. But is it necessary to do so? May a legend not lose its charm if subjected to analysis and dissection?

Legend has dwelt peacefully in Damascus, and has brought to that place numerous names, sacred and profane. Adam and Eve lived in Paradise, where life was easy, pleasant, and happy. As a result of their disobedience they were driven out of the Garden of Eden and forbidden to re-enter it. This story, thoroughly appreciated by the Arabs (who had experienced generally nothing but scorched lands), could find no

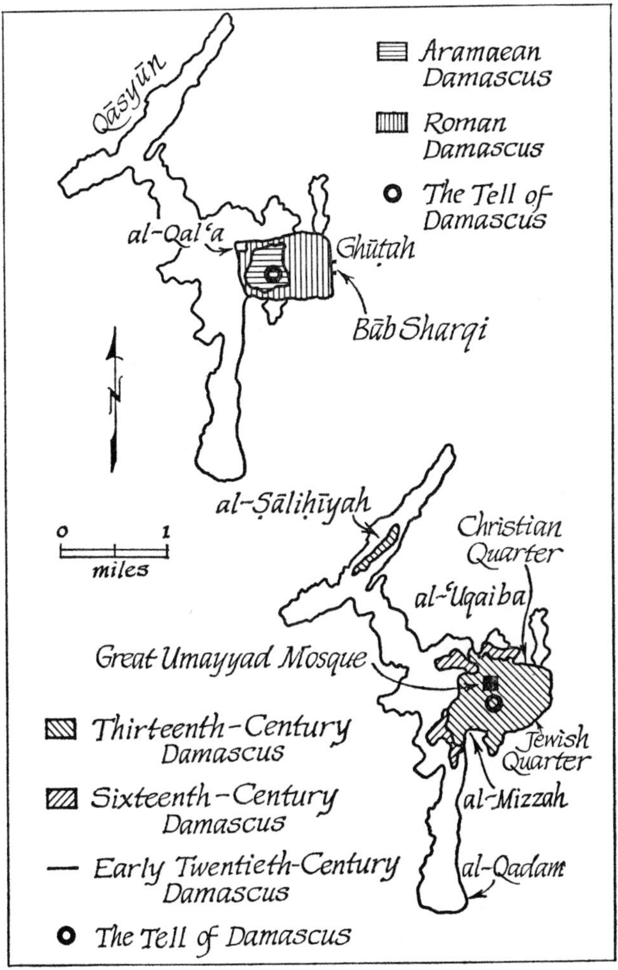

DAMASCUS
from Aramaean Times to the Twentieth Century

better place in which to settle than Damascus, and this town thus became Adam's original home. The reader may be reminded that Damascus was not the only place given this honor, but its locus in Damascus is what interests us at present.

The progeny of the father of the human race proved to be as jealous of each other as we are. One was a herdsman, while the other tilled the soil. The legend says that the two brothers placed their offerings before God, who accepted the fruits of the land proffered by Abel, but did not touch the gifts of the herdsman Cain. Cain, struck with anger, killed his brother. Jealousy was at the bottom of the murder; the needy, hardy shepherd was jealous of his well-to-do brother. Legend needed a place where a herdsman and a farmer could live close to each other, where the products of their work would differ greatly—to arouse jealousy. Damascus was accordingly suitable. The Ghūṭah provided the scene of lushness and wealth, while to the east, north, or south comparatively poor grazing ground was available. There was also a high place where offerings could be put, where the holy fire would descend and consume the one acceptable to the powers above. Hence Damascus was also the home of Cain and Abel.

The Qāsyūn, the mountain against which Damascus leans, was shocked by the fratricidal crime, and sent a cry through a cave which is still there. Abel's innocent blood could be seen, even in the twelfth century, on the rock where his brother slew him. Thus two witnesses to the cruelty of the deed constantly remind people of it. Adam was terribly grieved because of the loss of his son, and since there were no people to console him, he received such condolence from the angels, headed by Gabriel. The Cave of Gabriel was the place where Adam was comforted.

Abraham's father, Tarah, was, according to legend, a manufacturer of statues for worship, and Abraham, who had seen the light, knew better, so he destroyed his father's works. Someone sometime must have become conscious of the possibility of having within the area righteous persons as well as the ignorant. Tarah represented the latter, while Abraham stood for the former. They were both brought there and Damascus became the home of the two men, with Bait Laḥya, a suburb, as the specific site.

Christ and his mother were also brought to Damascus, at al-Rabwa. The Qur'ān (Koran) refers to them as having been settled on a hill with a copious spring of water. This beautiful suburban hill provided the proper surrounding, but to explain the whole question, legend arranged for the home of St. Anne, St. Mary's mother, to be transferred from Nazareth to al-Nayrab, in the neighborhood of Damascus. For Jesus and his mother to go there would then be natural—it was a visit to the ancestral home!

To the best of modern historical knowledge, Muḥammad, the Prophet of Islam, probably never set foot in Damascus, but legend carried him there. It was, however, cautious. He reached only al-Qadam, south of Damascus, where the trace of his foot, hence the name, was to be seen. As a child, I was shown something which people insisted was the footprint of the Prophet.

These legends grew with time; they were supported by *ḥadīths,* made especially and ascribed to the Prophet, to glorify the city. Centuries established both the *ḥadīths* and the legendary associations of Damascus, so that people accepted both. Popularly, the followers of each denomination are prepared to vouch for the truth of it all.

This is the Damascus whose story under the Mamlūks I propose to tell. It is a city which has left its imprint on its dwellers and visitors down to the present day. It has developed, it has changed, it has seen masters and it has overthrown masters—but two things in it seem to remain: an indomitable spirit and a charm.

Damascus

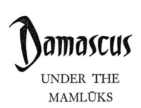

UNDER THE
MAMLŪKS

·1·

The Mamlūks

In the year 1171, Saladin, the trusted vizier of the Fatimid caliph in Cairo, put an end to this caliphate and proceeded to consolidate his own power in Egypt. He moved cautiously, for he could not afford to alienate his suzerain, Nūr al-Dīn of Damascus. The latter's death in 1174 left Saladin free. A journey to Syria late in the same year and an armed victory in the following one placed Muslim Syria under his domination. Preparations for a trial of strength with the Latin states were taken seriously by Saladin, and his victory against the armies of the Crusaders at the Battle of Ḥiṭṭīn, in 1187, increased his possessions. His death in 1193 at Damascus brought these active hostilities to a temporary halt.

Saladin founded an empire stretching from Mosul to the south of Egypt and established a dynasty which lasted until 1250. (In certain parts of Syria it lingered until the sixties or even later.) But his successors experienced periods of civil war and feudal struggle which weakened the kingdom, so much so that in 1229 al-Kāmil concluded a treaty with Frederick II, giving him Jerusalem, Bethlehem, and Nazareth.

The successors to the Ayyūbid sultanate of Saladin were the Mamlūks, who ruled over Egypt, Palestine, Lebanon, and Syria from 1250 until 1516–17, when they were defeated by the Ottomans.

The Mamlūks were slaves, purchased at the slave markets, and came from various races and locations. Their owner trained them in the arts of war, and they became his bodyguard. They established a military rule which continued for nearly three centuries. The throne was, generally speaking, the prize of personal prowess, courage, and daring, spiced with a great deal of intrigue. The ruling sultan, recognized by other Mamlūk chiefs only as *primus inter pares,* had to watch his supporters very carefully, for a change of allegiance and loyalty was not unusual in Mamlūk political behavior.

Not only the sultan but also each amir had his own bodyguard or personal army of slaves, which he paid out of his own private purse. As the sultan commanded larger sources of income, his entourage and supporters grew in number. His failure to please them, however, exposed him to deposition, exile, or even assassination.

The Ayyūbids had secured the approval and blessings of the 'Abbāsid caliph of Baghdad, a necessity which had developed throughout generations of Islamic experience of political expediency. The first Mamlūk sultan enjoyed this privilege, but the destruction of the caliphate by the Mongols in 1258 robbed the Mamlūks of such a concession. Feeling the need for having a caliph, Baybars (1260–76) brought a fugitive descendant of the 'Abbāsids who had escaped death to Cairo, where he was acclaimed caliph, thus reviving the caliphate in 1260. The caliph, in turn, delegated his authority, in his capacity as commander of the faithful, to the sultan; thus the caliph's office was, during the Mamlūk era, a sinecure. The sultan thought of himself as *ṣāḥib* (owner) of the kingdom, and his word was law throughout the realm. The Mamlūks remained a military aristocracy; they monopolized military offices, leaving judicial and clerical positions to be filled by native people—but of their own choice.

* * *

In consolidating their power, the Mamlūks had to think of facing the two most eminent dangers that threatened the area. On the one hand, the Crusaders were still in occupation of all the coastal parts of Palestine, Lebanon, and Syria; on the other, the Mongols were moving westward after their success against Baghdad and its rulers.

The conflicts with the Latins took the shape of concentrated and vehement Mamlūk attacks against weakening Crusader defenses. In 1291 the last Latin stronghold on the mainland fell to the Mamlūks. Three sultans were primarily responsible for bringing this about: Baybars, al-Nāṣir Qalāwūn (1279–90), and al-Ashraf Khalīl (1290–93). Details of the campaign fall outside the scope of the present work, but the reader should be reminded that the attacks were ruthless and that the destruction they left in their wake, especially in the coastal towns, paralyzed the area for generations.

The threat of the Mongols was more serious because their hordes were greater and their desire for combat and blood was insatiable. They kept appearing on the scene, destroying towns and cities, putting thousands of people to the sword, and carrying off skilled artisans to the central parts of Asia. However, the Mamlūks managed to divert the danger earlier, and later, in the fifteenth century, the wave of Mongol campaigns exhausted itself, at least in Syria.

The first defeat the Mongols sustained was in 1260, at the Battle of ʿAyn Jālūt in northern Palestine. Of the more serious and devastating expeditions that followed, two deserve special mention. In 1298–99, Ghāzān led his armies into Syria, captured numerous towns in the north, defeated a Mamlūk army under al-Nāṣir Muḥammad (near Ḥimṣ), and occupied Damascus. His troops looted the city, of whose population a large number, claimed to be 100,000, were put to the sword. Ghāzān, however, evacuated the city in 1300, leaving its administration to one of his representatives.

Ibn Kathīr, a historian of the fourteenth century, has left a vivid account of Ghāzān's attack on the city. The following is an abridged translation.

> In the year 699 [1298–99] news came that the Mongols were marching on Syria. People were frightened; and Aleppo and Hama were practically deserted. One paid 200 dirhams [$14.00] for an animal of burden from Hama to Damascus. However, good tidings came that the sultan had departed from Egypt to Syria. Nearly three months later he entered Damascus. In spite of heavy rains and mud, people went out to meet him, and the city was decorated for the occasion. The times were difficult, and the city was crowded with those who had fled their towns. The minister demanded special revenues; money was borrowed from orphans' and captives' funds to strengthen the army. After a sojourn of nine days the sultan led his armies, accompanied with volunteers, to

meet the Mongols. People in the city prayed and recited liturgies for victory. But at Wādi al-Khaznadār, near Hama, the Mongols defeated the Muslim army, and the sultan deserted the field of battle. . . . Many, many lives were lost. . . . The soldiers from Egypt returned home.

The Damascenes were frightened; Ghāzān was approaching their city. So some prominent members of the community, with Ibn Taymīyah at their head, went to Ghāzān at al-Nabk to secure an amnesty for the population. . . . On the following day, a Friday, the imam mentioned no names on the occasion of the prayers. . . . On Saturday the expected firman granting the Damascenes the amnesty was read at the mosque. On the next day horses, arms, and money were demanded by representatives of Ghāzān. As his forces approached the city, lawlessness again prevailed, and confiscations and looting became the order of the day. Arghwāsh, governor of the citadel, refused to surrender it.

Qabjaq was appointed Ghāzān's governor; but his soldiers continued to rob and loot and take away the women. It was estimated that about 400 people from al-Ṣāliḥīyah alone lost their lives. The same was repeated in al-Mizzah and many other suburbs.

Ibn Taymīyah tried to contact Ghāzān again, but in vain. The Mongols were now determined to occupy the citadel. They had already taken away about 10,000 horses, besides arms and money, so the defense of the citadel was not an easy task for the governor. The Mongols built their mangonel in the mosque to attack the citadel from its court. Having closed the gates of the mosques, the Mongols guarded the timber prepared for the mangonel. Arghwāsh, with the defense of the citadel in mind, destroyed most of the buildings around it. People, fearing *corvée* remained at home. Hardly anyone appeared in the streets, and the mosques were practically deserted. Confiscations of property and looting continued. But the citadel withstood the assault.

Ghāzān returned home, and Qabjaq was entrusted with the administration, a task which he took seriously and ceremoniously. He rode through the city and the suburbs with great pomp, dispatched his emissaries everywhere, and proclaimed his own decrees throughout the land. In order to increase the revenues he permitted drinking places and houses of prostitution to operate. The income from this was 1,000 dirhams [$70.00] per day. People in the villages and towns were exposed to the evils of lusty, unwieldy, and barbarous soldiery.

Eventually Qabjaq arranged for the Mongol soldiers to depart, declared the roads and markets safe. Soon news came that the sultan had left Cairo, so Qabjaq went out with his troops to prevent him from entering the city. Arghwāsh, the governor of the citadel, called upon the people of Damascus to shut the gates, man the walls, and be prepared. Ibn Taymīyah, with his men, went around closing drinking places and breaking the wine vessels. Bāb al-Faraj was later opened to admit the Mamlūks coming from Egypt, but the sultan had returned to Cairo.

Collaborators with the Mongols were severely punished, and rebellious people were brought to obedience. It became customary to hang arms in shops and markets, and students as well as others were to receive military training, in preparation to fight the enemy.

Year 700 [1299]: the Mamlūk tax collector now asked for revenues and loans. People were disturbed, but the amounts were collected all the same. News came that Ghāzān was keeping his promise to return to occupy Egypt. People were at a loss and more than ever were ready to leave Damascus for Egypt, but could not afford to pay for beasts of burden. Ibn Taymīyah was against this, and used his eloquence and powers of persuasion to stop this mass migration. His opinion was that the Mongols had annoyed God by their evil doings and killing other Muslims. His words worked a miracle; the exodus was stayed. News that the sultan had left Cairo for Syria encouraged people of the city.

The Mongols drew nearer, conquering the northern parts of Syria; people were again frightened, especially when news came that the sultan had returned to Cairo. So the exodus began again; parents carried their children through rain and mud and traveled long distances in hunger and weariness. Ibn Taymīyah again assumed the role of the savior. He went to the army, camped outside the wall, and exhorted the men to defend the city to the utmost of their abilities, assuring them that victory would be theirs. He was asked by the governor and his officers to go to Cairo to convince the sultan to lead his armies against the Mongols. Ibn Taymīyah accepted the mission and left immediately. Amongst other things, he told the sultan and his men, "If you do not want to protect our country, which happens to be under your authority, we would be prepared to have our own sultan, who would always be ready to defend the land. . . . Even had you not been the rulers of that part of the world, you should extend to it your protection."

Again Ibn Taymīyah succeeded and the armies were soon on the move. That year the Mongols did not continue their march to Damascus. It was in 702 [1300] that the Mongols again arrived in the north.

As the Egyptian army made no appearance on the scene, the inhabitants of Damascus began their southern trek to

Egypt and al-Karak. Although this stopped when the vanguard of the army from Egypt appeared, Damascus had to receive those who had run away from the north as the Mongols approached their cities and towns.

Eventually the armies left the immediate neighborhood of Damascus and encamped at al-Kiswah, to the south of the city, which gave rise to the rumors that they were pulling out and leaving the city to its fate. More people entered Damascus, hoping that the citadel and the walls might be better protection than the defecting soldiers. This gave robbers and evildoers an opportunity to rob, loot, and create havoc in the city. The situation improved when the sultan arrived at al-Kiswah.

The Mongols must have become quite disorderly by now [Ramaḍān, 702], so when the two armies met, they were defeated.

* * *

The second important invasion of Syria by the Mongols was led by Tīmūr (Tamerlane), who swept the country in 1402, devastating, killing, and ravaging as much as was humanly possible. Damascus, like areas to the north of it, fell to his sword. He withdrew because of Ottoman danger in the north, and only his death in 1405 saved Syria from another invasion. Tīmūr carried away with him the choice of Damascene scholars and the pick of its artisans, who beautified his capital, Samarqand, and planted Islamic sciences and learning in the very heart of Asia. The following is a summary translation of Ibn Taghri-Birdi's account of the fate of Damascus at the hands of Tīmūr.

On hearing that Tīmūr had captured Aleppo in northern

Syria, Sultan al-Nāṣir left Cairo [early 803/1402] with his troops and judges, while his governor of Cairo went about collecting more men and beasts of burden to send to the sultan's camp. The army then moved to Ghazzah. The sultan was advised that the people of Damascus and its army would be able to defend the city against Tīmūr, because they were numerous and the people were bitterly set against the Mongols on account of their earlier experiences with Ghāzān. Besides, the city was rich and it had provisions sufficient for one full year. But the sultan, and a few of his amirs, thought differently, so they marched toward Damascus, arriving there three months after their departure from Cairo. The Damascenes were overjoyed at the idea, and received the sultan with prayers to God for his victory. After a short rest at the citadel, the sultan led his men to the fields outside the city in preparation for Tīmūr. A skirmish actually took place, in which the sultan's men were victorious; thus they felt quite confident of victory.

Soon Tīmūr arrived and camped to the north of the city. A minor battle took place and again Tīmūr's men suffered a defeat, and numerous amirs, on both sides, were taken captives. Tīmūr then asked to negotiate for peace, but his request was rejected.

Soon after this a number of the high-ranking Egyptian amirs disappeared. It was rumored later that they went to Egypt to arrange for the deposition of al-Nāṣir, who soon left with some of his trusted followers. Those remaining in Damascus resumed their intrigues, feuds, and rivalry, forgetting that Tīmūr was threatening their very existence; most of them departed later for Egypt. So the people of Damascus "were left as a shepherdless herd." The Damascene soldiery, aided by the men of the city and those who had joined them from Aleppo, Hama, and other places, were determined to defend their "city." They, well armed, mounted the walls, and repulsed the vanguard of Tīmūr's attackers, who suffered great losses. Tīmūr then announced that he wanted peace with the city and that he was prepared to grant amnesty to the people. This appealed to a besieged populace, who delegated the chief justice of Damascus to negotiate with the great Mongol. Tīmūr impressed the man, saying that he "approached Damascus only to punish Sodon, the Mamlūk governor, who has killed a number of my [Tīmūr's] men. Sodon is now in my hands; so I have no grudge against the city of prophets and companions, and I have given it in alms for my sons. . . . I want to return home, but before that I will have to collect the gifts and presents." These Tīmūr called *tuqquzāt,* that is, the "nines" of each commodity [the Turkish word *tuqquz* means "nine"].

Negotiations went on, with more people joining the chief justice. By the time Tīmūr was financially appeased the Damascenes had paid him ten million pieces [$1,000,000] collected by various ways and means from everyone in the city. Then Tīmūr demanded that the city surrender all arms, irrespective of whether they belonged to the army or the civilian population. The only group that resisted were those in the citadel, who managed to burn the first tower built by Tīmūr's men, but had to surrender when overwhelmed by a larger number of attackers with better arms.

Having secured all that, Tīmūr declared his amnesty null and void, divided the *ḥārahs* [quarters] of the city amongst his amirs, who entered it with their courtiers, collected more money, inflicted more punishment on the people, using all brutal means, including burning people alive and hanging others by their heads from the battlements of the walls. They then proceeded to abduct women and younger boys, abusing them publicly. . . . The people of Damascus never experienced anything like that in their long history.

When the amirs had satisfied their desires, they left the city. Then Tīmūr gave Damascus to his men, who repeated the same things with more savagery and brutality. They took with them all males of over five years, and then they set fire to the city, which lasted for three days and nights.

Thus Tīmūr, who had laid siege to the city for eighty days, departed northward, having destroyed the noble Damascus—walls, houses, *qaysariyas,* baths, and, above all, mosques. The city was in ruins inhabited only by children.

The Mamlūks also waged a war against the Shīʿite strongholds in Syria and the Maronite areas in Lebanon. In addition, they carried their arms into Armenia on more than one occasion.

The political domination of the Middle East was contested, in the late fifteenth and early sixteenth centuries, by the Persians, the Turks, and Mamlūks. The Mamlūks had already exhausted themselves and the people of their empire, the Persians were too far away to descend on the western parts of the Fertile Crescent, but the Turks were both capable and willing. Selim I of Turkey led his armies against al-Ghawri, next to the last of the Mamlūk sultans, who was defeated and killed near Aleppo in 1516. Syria, Lebanon, and Palestine lay at the feet of the Ottoman conqueror. Al-Ghawri's successor, Ṭūmān-bāy, was defeated near Cairo early in 1517, and Egypt became an Ottoman province. The Mamlūks disappeared as a political power.

The Mamlūks became acquainted with the use of firearms

sometime in the sixties of the fourteenth century. In the fifteenth, they were producing their own firearms, as attested by Ibn Taghri-Birdi. But the Mamlūk sultans restricted the use of artillery to siege warfare, and never used it in battles. Apparently, the employment of *madāfi'* (guns) for siege and defense purposes did not demand any drastic changes in the military structure of the army, based essentially on men bought in the slave market and trained to the use of the sword and, later, and to a limited extent, the musket. This structure could not accommodate artillery, and the Mamlūks were neither psychologically nor socially prepared to change their own military organization to suit the new weapons.

The last Mamlūk sultans realized the danger of the Ottomans in the north and encouraged the manufacture of guns. Ibn Taghri-Birdi gives an interesting description of guns and tests which belong to the time of Khushqadam. The following is a partial translation (abridged from Ayalon):

> And on Tuesday the fourteenth of Shawwāl, 868 [1464], the Sultan Khushqadam gave an order to test the firing capacity of the royal cannon [*al-midfa' al-sulṭānī*] which the master artificer Ibrāhīm al-Ḥalabī had cast for him in the Cairo citadel. Earlier, at the end of Ramaḍān, the cannon had already been tested once in the presence of the sultan, firing several rounds. At the time of that test the cannon had been mounted under the walls of the citadel and had fired in the direction of the Red Mountain. Afterward it was transferred to the foot of al-Jabal al-Aḥmar and was mounted on a high wall . . . outside Cairo. . . . On Thursday the ninth of the month [i.e., Shawwāl] it was tested for the second time, firing several rounds in the presence of a big crowd and a group of

> amirs . . . and other high personages of the realm. . . . When the above-mentioned Tuesday [i.e., the fourteenth of Shawwāl] arrived, the cannon was tested for the third time from the same place. . . . It was fired twice.

Al-Ghawri faced the Ottoman danger personally. He ordered an increase in the casting of cannons, but apparently only for defense and siege purposes. In order to put his armies on equal footing with the Ottoman invader, he revived *furūsīyah,* or horsemanship, giving his cavalry chances for more and better training. He recognized, however, that Ottoman fighters depended on firearms, so he reinforced the troops using harquebuses, who were men of lower social standing than his Mamlūk knights and were sometimes even black slaves.

What al-Ghawri did not, or could not, realize was that the Ottoman soldiers had field artillery to protect and support their advances, so when he faced the armies of Selim I at Marj Dābiq, near Aleppo, his men, although fighting gallantly, were no match for the "firing engines." The Mamlūks, to a certain extent, suffered defeat there and near Cairo because they could not conceive the great change that the use of artillery on the field of battle meant to an army. The Ottoman victory was, in addition to other factors, a victory of new tactics and weapons.

* * *

The Mamlūks were great builders, as is attested by the architectural monuments which adorn Cairo and other cities. They were interested in schools and they encouraged learning to a degree unexpected from a group of people of their background and occupation. The lands under their domination continued to be the crossroads of trade and commerce, as they had been for centuries, and thus continued to supply Mamlūk greed with high dividends from commerce. But the Mamlūks did not give farmers of Syria and Palestine a respite or encouragement to develop their agricultural activities to the full. When, thus, trade routes shifted to South Africa late in the fifteenth century, the Mamlūks did not have much to depend on for their needs, and the people suffered greatly.

It must be added that the area suffered a serious epidemic during the sultanate of Barsbāy (1422–38) which, although not as bad as the Black Death of Europe, was bad enough to affect the economic and social structure of the countries concerned. Ibn Taghri-Birdi, one of the best-known chroniclers of the period, gives a vivid account of the plague. "It began at Aleppo," he says, "then it spread throughout al-Shām. The people of the regions of Ṣafad, Jerusalem, al-Karak, Nablus, and the coast suffered greatly; so did the *urbān* [nomads] of the desert. Only one old woman survived in Jenin, and she ran away. Similar things happened at Ramleh and other places. The *ḥānas* [hostelries] were full of corpses. . . . In Aleppo, 500 died in one day, and Damascus lost 1,200 per day in Rajab, 749."

* * *

Under the Mamlūks the area covering Palestine, Lebanon, and Syria was divided into six provinces, each referred to as a *mamlaka* (literally "kingdom"). That of Damascus was the largest, comprising central Syria, most of Palestine, and most of the area to the east of the river Jordan. Even parts of the Lebanese coast were under the jurisdiction of its governor. The province was centrally administered, so that even minor problems were discussed and decided in Damascus.

Generally speaking, there were three categories of government officials who dealt with the affairs of the province under the leadership of *nāyib al-ṣalṭana,* the governor. These divisions were named after the duties performed by them. At the top were officers of the sword (including commanders of the army and security forces), collectors of taxes and revenues, and supervisors of the *barīd* (postal service). These were all, without exception, of the Mamlūk aristocratic military caste. Next came the *dīwānī* (clerical) officers, whose duties had a civilian nature or who acted as the recorders and bookkeepers of the former group. Some of these officials were Mamlūks, but natives were equally eligible for these posts. The third category, and by no means the least important, was made up of religious officials, who supervised the administration of justice according to the Sharia and the maintenance of markets, undertook teaching in various schools, *zāwiyas* (convents), and mosques, and superintended the *bīmāristāns* (hospitals). These officers, except two, namely, the superintendent of the *qal'a* (citadel) and the chief justice of the province, were under the jurisdiction of the *nāyib al-ṣalṭana.* The sultan never trusted his lieutenants fully, so the citadel in Damascus (and in Aleppo) had its own garrison, where the commander was appointed by and directly responsible to the sultan in Cairo.

The administration of justice had always enjoyed a special position in Islam and had almost always been free from local administrative prejudices, so it had been the prerogative of the head of the state to appoint the higher judicial dignitaries. This tradition was followed by the Mamlūks. This did not mean that judges under the Mamlūks were always free from local pressures, but the stipulation gave them some moral support. Clashes between judges and governors were numerous, and some governors managed to have a judge dismissed by the sultan. Altogether, however, justice had at least theoretical protection.

The armies were of two kinds: the regulars, known as men of the *ḥalqa* (inner circle), and the personal bodyguard of the governor. To both must be added volunteers and conscripts during periods of need or pressure. It has been estimated that the Mamlūks could muster as many as 45,000 to 60,000 men at most, and it would be a force composed of all racial elements available in the area.

The taxes and revenues of the province, like the finances of the Mamlūk Empire itself, included *ḳharāj* (a land tax), *zaḳāh* (alms), *jizyah* (a poll tax paid by non-Muslim communities), the income of state domains, and *'ushūr* (customs). There were also numerous irregular taxes, imposed at the pleasure of the sultan; confiscations, of whose imposition even governors were capable; and requests, thought of on the spur of the moment.

Expenditures included the expenses of administrative and military machinery, the postal system, care and drainage of rivers and canals, and the maintenance of bridges and walls.

* * *

Abundance of water and a commanding position favored

the long-continuing existence of Damascus; political conditions determined its shape and form. In the eleventh century, political chaos, verging on anarchy, prevailed in Syria. Civil wars, intensive feuds, and nomadic raids forced people to seek security and safety inside the walls. Hence suburbs, already in existence earlier, were practically neglected by Damascenes. The walls of Damascus were the concern of the Saljūq governor, the *jāmiʿ* (congregational) mosque continued to be the meeting place par excellence, and the markets provided the inhabitants of the city with provisions and a place for gossip, but otherwise, "the city appeared as a collection of independent *ḥārahs,* each having its own peculiar life, separate from that of its neighbor. Each of those *ḥārahs* was a miniature town, with its own mosque, its own system for the distribution of water, its baths, its market which contained its needs. . . . The houses of the *ḥārah* could be reached only through its main entrance, the gate of which could be locked at night."

On many occasions, the citizens of Damascus had to organize themselves for the defense of the city. This took the form of "corporational movement." Each *ḥārah* had its own group of *aḥdāth* (youths), with their shaikh, or leader, who was responsible for their discipline. When the general welfare of the city was at stake, the *aḥdāth* went into common action. Thus the corporations served two purposes. On the one hand, they protected their members professionally against competition and also against the oppression of the governor. On the other, the corporations constituted their members, the *aḥdāth,* into a guard to defend the city. Sometime in the eleventh century, Banu al-Sūfī acquired hereditary title to the office of *ra'īs* (head) of a town, to which was added the shaikhship of the *aḥdāth*. In this case, the individual "represented the interests of the town, defended it against external danger, and mediated, supported with power, between the governor, who often shut himself in his citadel, and the corporation of the people." Damascus ceased to be an integrated personality or an active organism. It was a collection of individuals with contradicting interests, each of whom attended to his own benefits within his private zone, utilizing all circumstances for his personal ends, irrespective of the interests of his neighbors. But Damascus, so socially and politically rent, was economically active and fairly prosperous.

With the advent of the Zangids and Ayyūbids, in the twelfth century, law and order were partly restored to the land, and because of the impact of the Crusaders, rulers of Syria took matters seriously. Damascus, being a capital, received a great deal of attention. The city walls and the citadel were strongly fortified, the latter being enlarged to become not only a last place of defense for a besieged garrison but to include the sultan's residence, stores of provisions and ammunition, the mint, and the prison. It also had its own *jāmi'* mosque, baths, and *sūqs* (markets). Ibn Jubayr, a Muslim traveler from Spain who visited Damascus at the time of Saladin, wrote of the citadel: "Damascus has a castle where the Sultan lives. It stands apart, to the west of the city opposite Bāb al-Faraj [Gate of Consolation], one of the city's gates. The Sultan's congregational mosque is there, and the Friday service is held in it."

The restoration of law and order in the twelfth century

improved economic conditions; Damascus benefited from this both commercially and industrially, and its population increased. Internally, however, the city did not change much. Streets remained narrow and crowded, *ḥārahs* continued to be the basis of professional and religious social life, but the corporations were placed under strict surveillance. They were considered, and not completely wrongly, either, possible channels through which a suppressed populace voiced grievances through Shī'ism, which from the sultan's view was dangerous to the Sunnite state.

People no longer felt the necessity of residing inside the walls of Damascus; hence the almost revolutionary development of the suburbs, which was matched only by the growth of economic activity in the city. Both aspects of Damascene life continued throughout the thirteenth, fourteenth, and fifteenth centuries.

* * *

The Mamlūks watched their provinces more closely and enforced law and order more rigorously. Under the new regime, Damascus continued to develop along the lines and trends which had already been outlined. It was, to the Mamlūks, their first city after Cairo, and a military center. More suburbs were added, particularly in connection with the army. One such new area was Maydān Taḥt al-Qal'a (Citadel Square), which included the markets of horse dealers, saddlers, and other leather workers. Tanners were also accommodated there. Adjoining this, to the north of it, Sūq Ṣārūja grew enormously. Of the more residential quarters which developed during the thirteenth and fourteenth centuries, al-Ṣāliḥīyah is the best example. It was just another town outside the city walls.

Damascenes have always enjoyed picnicking in the vicinity of their city. During the period under consideration, more permanent centers for pleasure and merriment came to exist—the Ghūṭah, al-Rabwa, Wādi al-Banafsaj, Bayn al-Nahrayn, and al-Yalakī are among the best-known places.

One of the most interesting features of Damascus is the large number of *madrasas* (schools) it had during that era, not that Damascus had not been a center of learning earlier in its history, but the school was especially emphasized under the Zangids, Ayyūbids, and Mamlūks. The appearance of these regimes signalized a revival of Sunnite authority and a defeat for Shī'ism, which had been fairly widespread in Syria. The school, as first instituted by the Saljūqs, was, more or less, under government supervision. With the Ayyūbids, it became an instrument for combating Shī'ism and upholding the official Sunnite religious views. Rulers founded schools and encouraged others to found them. In all cases, schools were richly endowed.

·2·

The Damascus of Saladin and Ibn Jubayr

LATE IN THE MORNING of July 5, 1184, Ibn Jubayr, a Spanish Muslim traveler of great renown, arrived in Damascus. Approaching it from the north, he beheld an impressive view of a magnificent city surrounded with extensive gardens of deep green and streams glittering in the sun. A master of Arabic style, Ibn Jubayr later described the scene which had vividly imprinted itself upon his mind in the following words:

> Damascus is the paradise of the Orient and dawning place of her gracious and resplendent beauty. She is "on a hill having meadows and springs" with deep shade and delicious water. Its rivulets twist like serpents through every way, and the perfumed zephyrs of its flower gardens breathe life into the soul. To those who contemplate her she displays herself in bridal dress, calling to them: "Come to the halting place of beauty, and take midday repose."
>
> Its ground is sickened with the superfluity of water, so that it yearns even for a drought, and the hard stones almost cry out to you: "Stamp with thy foot; here is a cool spring for thee to wash thyself and to drink." [Koran XXXVIII, 42].

> The gardens encircle it like the halo round the moon and contain it as it were the calyx of a flower. To the east, its green Ghūṭah stretches as far as the eye can see, and wherever you look on its four sides its ripe fruits hold the gaze. By Allah, they spoke truth who said, "If Paradise be on earth it is Damascus without a doubt; and if it be in Heaven, Damascus is its earthly counterpart and equivalent."

Ibn Jubayr was not just a traveler, but a learned Muslim who, before coming to Damascus, had visited Egypt and Iraq and had performed the sacred pilgrimage. He journeyed with open eyes and ears and was interested in Muslim learning, schools, mosques, *zāwiyas,* and various other aspects of life in the places he visited. If we accompany Ibn Jubayr throughout his visit to Damascus, in which he spent a little over two months, we shall have a picture of the city as it was in the times of Saladin, shortly before the Mamlūks took over, established rigorous law and order, and thus encouraged people to settle widely outside the walls of the city. He tells us that the walled city was not excessively big, that

> its streets were narrow and dark, and its houses were made of mud and reeds, arranged in three storeys one over the other so that fire speedily took hold of them. Damascus contained as many as three cities, for it was the most populous in the world. Its beauty was all outside, not in. The markets of Damascus were the finest in the world and the best arranged, and the most handsomely constructed. Especially was this so with the *qaysariyas* which were tall as caravanserias and furnished with iron gates like those of a castle. Each *qaysariya* was distinguished by its shape and iron gates. The city had another market called al-Sūq al-Kabīr [the Great

> Market] which extended from Bāb al-Jābiya to Bāb Sharqi [along the "Street Called Straight"].

Damascus also attracted the attention of Benjamin of Tudela, who visited the city in 1163 and wrote:

> This city is very large and handsome, and is inclosed with a wall and surrounded by a beautiful country, which in a circuit of fifteen miles presents the richest gardens and orchards, in such numbers and beauty as to be without equal upon earth. The rivers Amana and Parpar, the sources of which came from the Mount on which the city leans, run down here; the Amana follows its course through Damascus, and its waters are carried by means of pipes into the streets and markets. A considerable trade is carried on here by merchants of all countries. The Parpar runs between the gardens and orchards in the outskirts, and supplies them copiously with water.

As a pious Muslim, Ibn Jubayr found great joy in the *jāmiʿ* mosque, built originally by the Umayyads and named for them. He spent many hours in it, described it at length and in great detail, climbed its dome, and mentioned all of its venerated sites and places. The Great Umayyad Mosque has always been the most magnificent landmark of the city, and it is worthwhile to pay a short visit to it in the company of Ibn Jubayr:

> For beauty, perfection of construction, marvellous and sumptuous embellishment and decoration, it is one of the most celebrated mosques of the world. Its general fame in this regard renders valueless a deep description. One of the strangest things concerning it is that the spider never spins

his web therein, nor do swallows ever enter it or alight thereon.

Its measurement in length, from east to west, is two hundred paces, which is equivalent to three hundred cubits; and its measurement in width from south to north is one hundred and thirty-five paces, which is equivalent to two hundred cubits. Its area in the Maghribi maraja' [fifty square cubits] is twenty-four maraja', which is the same area as that of the mosque of God's Prophet—may God bless and preserve him—in Medina, except that lengthways the latter extends from south to north. The aisles along the south side are three in number and stretch from east to west, and the breadth of each aisle is eighteen paces, a pace being a cubit and a half.

The aisles are raised on sixty-eight supports: fifty-four of these are pillars, eight are stucco pilasters interspersed between the pillars, two are marble-covered pilasters set with them into the wall that adjoins the court, and four are piers that are covered with marble in a most beautiful fashion, being studded with coloured marble mosaics arranged in rings, and illustrated with *miḥrābs* [niches] and rare designs.

A colonnade, ten paces wide, runs round the court on three sides, the east, the west, and the north. . . . The number of gilt and stained-glass windows is seventy-four.

The blessed congregational mosque, both inside and out, is inlaid with gilded mosaics, is embellished with the most superb architectural ornament, and is miraculously executed. Twice it suffered fire and was destroyed and twice rebuilt. Most of its marble went, and its splendour changed. The parts best preserved today are the qiblah [southern] side and the three cupolas alongside it. Its *miḥrāb* is the most wonderful in Islam for its beauty and rare art, and the whole of it gleams with gold. Within it are small *miḥrābs* adjoining its wall and surrounded by small columns, voluted like a bracelet as if done by a turner, than which nothing more beautiful could be seen, some of them being red as coral. The glory of the qiblah of this blessed mosque and the three cupolas adjoining it, irradiated by the gilded and coloured windows whose very colour is reflected on the qiblah wall as the rays of the sun pour through them, is such as to dazzle the eyes.

In the blessed mosque there are many zāwiyas used by students for copying [the Koran] and for study and for withdrawal from the press of men; and they are amongst the advantages provided for students. In the wall abutting on the court and enclosed by the south colonnade there are, throughout its length, twenty doors surmounted by stuccoed arches, the whole with hollowed moundings in the form of windows; and in their unbroken continuity the eyes perceive the most beautiful and graceful spectacle. As to the colonnades that enclose the court from [the other] three sides, they are supported by columns over which are arched embrasures sustained by smaller columns that go round the whole of the court. This court is one of the most beautiful and splendid of sights. Here the population congregate, for it is their place of care-dispelling and recreation, and here every evening you will see them, coming and going from east to west, from Bāb Jairūn to Bāb al-Barīd [the Gate of the Postal Service], and others you will see talking to their friends, and some reading. In this manner they will go on, coming and going, until the end of the last evening prayers, and then depart. Some do this in the morning, but the largest assembly is in the evening, and he who surveys it will conceive it to be the night of the twenty-seventh of Ramaḍān the venerated for what he will observe of the multitude of people congregating together. They do not cease from doing this every day. The idle ones among men call them "ploughmen."

In this venerated mosque, after the morning prayers, there daily assembles a great congregation for the reading of the Koran. This is unfailing, and it is the same after the evening prayers. To this assembly come all who do not well know the Koran by heart; and all such participants receive a daily allowance, more than five hundred persons being able to live from it. This is one of the virtues of this venerated mosque, in which from morn till eve the Koran is read unceasingly. In it lectures are delivered to students, and the teachers receive a liberal stipend. The Malikites have a zāwiya for study in the west side, and there the students from the Maghrib, who receive a fixed allowance, assemble. The conveniences of this venerated mosque for strangers and students are indeed many and wide.

The mosque has three minarets. One on the west side is like a lofty tower with large apartments and spacious chapels, all leading to large doors and lived in by strangers of pious mode of life.

The most impressive thing in this blessed mosque is the Lead Dome in the centre of the building beside the *miḥrāb*. It rises high into the air with a vast circumference, and is supported by the huge erection which is the nave and which extends from the *miḥrāb* to the court.

One of the grandest and most remarkable sights in the world, amongst its imposing edifices of miraculous art and perfection, and admitted to be beyond description even in the most eloquent of tongues, is achieved by climbing to the top of the Lead Dome in the centre of the congregational mosque, and entering into its interior, and then turning a reflective gaze on its superb structure, with the cupola poised within it like a hollow sphere inside another larger than itself.

Inside this cupola as seen from the interior of the venerated mosque, are wooden panels fitted together and joined in wondrous fashion. They are all gilded in the most beautiful form of that work, adorned with many colours, exquisitely carved, dazzling the eyes with the refulgence of the gold.

Not much less enchanting to Ibn Jubayr were the schools, hospitals, and *zāwiyas* in Damascus. To him, these were places of Muslim learning, social solidarity, and philanthropy. His zeal is certainly clear in his description of them:

> There are about twenty colleges in the city, and two hospitals, one old and the other new. The new is the finer and bigger, and receives a daily allowance of about fifteen dinars. It has a staff who maintain a register that records the names of the sick and the items they require of medicine, food, and other things. Early each morning the physicians come to the hospital to visit the sick and order the preparation of the proper medicines and food according as suits each person. The other hospital is managed in the same way, but more people use the new. The old one stands west of the venerated mosque. There is also a system of treatment for confined lunatics, and they are bound in chains. We take refuge in God from this trial and sore affliction.
>
> These hospitals are among the great glories of Islam, and so are the colleges. One of the finest looking colleges in the world is that of Nūr al-Dīn—may God's mercy rest upon his soul—and in it is his tomb—may God illumine it. It is a sumptuous palace. Water pours into it through an aqueduct in the middle of a great canal, filling an oblong fountain and finally falling into a large cistern in the centre of the building. The eyes are enchanted by the beauty of the sight, and all who see it renew their supplications for Nūr al-Dīn—may God's mercy rest upon his soul.

> As for the convents which they call *khawāniq,* they are many and are used by the Ṣūfis. They are elaborately decorated palaces, with water flowing to all their parts forming the most agreeable sight one could see. The members of these orders of Ṣūfis are the kings of these parts, for God has sufficed them of the goods and favours of the world, and freed them from thoughts of winning their livelihood that they might apply them to His worship, lodging them in palaces that remind them of the palaces of heaven. Those happy ones of them who have received God's help, enjoy, by His grace, the favours of this world and the next. They follow a noble path, and their social conduct is admirable. The style of their ritual in worship is remarkable, and excellent is their custom of assembling to listen to impassioned music. In these ecstasied and abstracted states the world forsakes them, such is their rapture and transport. In a word, all their affairs are wonderful, and they hope for a future life of bliss and felicity.

Needless to say, Ibn Jubayr did not confine his activities or descriptions to the city inside the walls. He moved about, enjoyed himself, and visited venerated places for the sake of blessings. By his time, Damascus had already become an integral part of religious folklore in Islam. The Umayyads (661–750), and others after them, had gradually given Damascus a sanctified position—as the place where Cain killed Abel, where Abraham was born, where the head of John the Baptist was buried, and, last but not least, where the Virgin Mary and Jesus found refuge. To this should be added the fact that the city's cemeteries contained the tombs of numerous companions of the Prophet. Some were actually buried there, but to Damascus was ascribed the honor of having more than its share of such graves. Ibn Jubayr went to all of these places and felt the joy of being able to do so. He also visited places of beauty: the suburbs of Damascus. We have already seen his description of the citadel. Let us now follow him to the area immediately next to it, the place which in the thirteenth century would come to be known as Maydān Taḥt al-Qalʿa:

> Fast by it [the citadel] and outside the city are two horse-courses, so green as to seem to be rolls of silk brocade. They are enclosed by a wall, with the river running between them, and bordering them is a large wood of poplars forming a very pleasant sight. The Sultan goes out to them to play sawalajān [a variety of polo], and to race his horses. There is no place like them for the eye to wander in. Every evening the Sultan's sons visit them to practise archery, race horses, and play sawalajan.

Ibn Jubayr climbed Qāsyūn, the mountain to the west of Damascus, from which he viewed the city and its suburbs. His description certainly gives us a picture of late twelfth century Damascus and an idea of the legends attached to it. He wrote:

> At the top of the mountain is a grotto called the Grotto of Adam—may God bless and preserve him—which has a building over it and is a blessed spot. Below, at the foot of the mountain, is another called the Cave of Hunger where it is said that seventy prophets died of hunger. They had possessed one loaf that they continued to press on each other, pass-it from hand to hand until fate overtook them—God's blessings upon them. Over this cave too has been built a mosque in which we saw lamps that are lit [night and] day. To all these shrines are attached endowments consisting of gardens, arable lands, and houses, to the extent that all that is in the country

is almost wholly comprised of these pious bequests. For every mosque, school, or convent newly erected, the Sultan will assign to it a religious endowment that will support it and those that dwell therein as well as its officials. These also are among the generous deeds that are enduring. Amongst the princesses who possess the means, some order the building of a mosque, or an asylum for the poor, or a school, spending on them large sums, and assigning to them endowments from their properties; and there are Emirs who do the same. In this blessed path they reveal a readiness to do good that will be rewarded by Great and Glorious God.

At the edge of this mountain, where the western plain with its gardens comes to an end, is the blessed hill mentioned in the Book of God Most High [Koran XXIII, 50] as being the dwelling of the Messiah and his mother—God's blessings upon them both. It is one of the most remarkable sights in the world for beauty, elegance, height, and perfection of construction, for the embellished plaster-work, and for the glorious site. It is like a towering castle, and one climbs to it by steps. The blessed dwelling is a small grotto in its middle, like a small chamber, and beside it is another room said to be the oratory of al-Khiḍr [Elijah]—may God bless and preserve him. Men hasten forward to pray at these two blessed spots, especially in the blessed dwelling. This has an iron door that closes on it. The mosque encloses the hill, where there are circular paths and a fountain than which no more beautiful could be seen. Water is brought to it from the top of the hill, and pours into a conduit in the wall that is connected with a marble basin, into which the water falls. A better sight could not be seen. Behind the fountain are ablution places into every room of which runs water, which flows round the side adjoining the wall that has the conduit.

This blessed hill is the limit of the town's gardens, and the dividing place of its water which here forms seven tributaries, each one taking its own way. The largest of these is called Thawra, and it passes under the hill, through whose base it has cut through the hard stone until it has opened an underground course wide like a cave. Sometimes a boy or man, being a bold swimmer, will plunge from the hill-top into the river and then will be pushed along by the current under the water until he passes through the channel beneath the hill and comes out at its foot on the other side. It is indeed a great hazard.

From this hill one may look over all the western gardens of the town, and there is no prospect like it for beauty, comeliness, and spacious vista. And below it flow these seven rivers, passing through divers ways and entrancing the eyes with the beauty of their joinings and separations and their gush and flow. The nobility of the site of this hill, and all its beauties, are greater than a describer can comprehend even in the highest flights of his praise. Amongst the famous places of the world its state is eminent and commanding.

Close to the foot of the hill is a large village called al-Nayrab, which is hidden in the gardens, for only the tops of its buildings are seen. It has a congregational mosque of unsurpassed beauty whose roof is wholly set with mosaics of many coloured marbles which the beholder would conceive to be a carpet of silk brocade. It has a fountain of exquisite beauty and a place of ablution with ten doors and water running in it and around it. Above this village, to the south, lies a considerable village, and one of the finest, called al-Mizzah, which has a large congregational mosque and a fountain of spring water. Al-Nayrab has a bath, as indeed have most of the villages of Damascus.

·3·

European Travelers in Damascus

In 1250 the Mamlūks established themselves in Egypt and within half a century they had added all Palestine, Lebanon, and Syria to their empire, thereby gaining control of the Latin states on the coast and liquidating Ayyūbid pockets in the interior. A stronger hand now ruled the area. Hence the tendency to expand, which Damascus had experienced late in the twelfth century, was now enhanced. Early in the fourteenth century, business activity shifted from the narrow streets of the walled city to the rapidly developing Maydān Taḥt al-Qalʿa, and the latter began to play a leading role in the city's economic life. Not only that, but economic activity increased generally because more and more of the surrounding region depended on Damascus and because the city was receiving an ever-increasing number of pilgrims who considered Damascus a rendezvous for caravans bound for Mecca. Thus a large number of people had to be provided for, not only during their sojourn in Damascus, but also for the lengthy journey to Mecca and back, which usually required three to four months. Since the route between Damascus and the Holy

Cities passed through barren deserts and since the Ḥijāz was a poor country, the pilgrims had to carry sufficient provisions for both the round trip and their stay in Mecca. Then, too, Damascus became a military base for the numerous expeditions which the Mamlūk sultans conducted against the Mongols, the Crusaders, the Armenians, and local rebels. Soldiers needed provisions, beasts of burden, equipment, and clothes. Damascus could only prosper in such circumstances.

The Mamlūks were lovers of building, and some of their architectural monuments in Damascus, such as the Ẓāhirīya School, delight the eyes even now. This helped masons and other skilled craftsmen to sustain the long-held tradition of decorative arts. Schools were numerous during the course of Mamlūk rule, and there was serious participation in education throughout that era.

As the population was encouraged to move outside the walls, older suburbs grew and new ones developed. Many became small towns.

The citadel grew in importance, especially as it became independent of the governor of the province of Damascus and had its own governor. An important part of the defense system of Damascus as early as the eleventh century, the citadel was the concern of the Zangids, the Ayyūbids, and the Mamlūks. Al-Ādil, uncle and successor of Saladin, perceived the need for its expansion and rebuilding. He almost razed the old structure, then made the amirs responsible for the new citadel, which had strong walls, twelve towers, and a moat. Baths, a school, a congregational mosque, and a pond were but a few of its features; gradually, houses for amirs, soldiers, and servants were built within its walls.

The citadel was almost in ruins by the time Ghāzān left Damascus. Al-Ẓāhir could not afford to leave the city defenseless, so he rebuilt its walls and attended to the reconstruction of the citadel. When completed, it had four gates, one of which, the eastern, opened toward the city, with a drawbridge spanning the moat. The remaining three led to areas outside the city, the western to the *sawalajān* grounds known as al-Maydān al-Akhḍar. Sinjir, governor of Damascus under al-Ashraf late in the thirteenth century, erected more buildings inside the walled area of the citadel and destroyed some of the houses and shops in the part of the city adjoining it. This probably marks the beginning of administrative separation between the citadel and the city.

Damascus and its citadel were battered by Tīmūr's armies, but they were soon rebuilt. The sultans could not afford to neglect such an important part of their fortifications.

European travelers were invariably impressed with the citadel. "At the end of the city," wrote Niccolo of Poggibonsi in the middle of the fourteenth century, "there is a strong castle with a high wall and by a bridge enters a river [moat], and it is guarded by the sultan." A little later, Giorgio Gucci described it in these words:

> Damascus, that is, the walled part, is in size about three times as large as Florence; and it is very well [enclosed] with two walls; that is, first, a wall about XXX braccia high which is very stout and stands on an outside moat, and then another wall, distant from the first about XV to XVI braccia, X braccia higher than the first: and both walls are embattled. At very frequent intervals, every L braccia, there are round towers, higher than the walls, and the said walls have two

> deep moats, one on the outside and one on the inside: and the said city in walls and moats is very strong, and inside there is a sort of citadel, about a mile in circumference, also with great moats and very high walls. And there dwell only men-at-arms who on behalf of the Sultan defend the city and the country; and nobody else is allowed there: and the dwelling is so large that it would take about XX thousand men-at-arms, all on horses.

Bertrandon de la Brocquiere, who visited Damascus after the siege of Tīmūr, said of it:

> Damascus has a strong castle on the side toward the mountain, with wide and deep ditches, over which the sultan appoints a captain of his own friends, who never suffers the governor to enter it. It was, in 1400, destroyed and reduced to ashes by Tamerlane. Vestiges of this disaster now remain; and toward the gate of St. Paul there is a whole quarter that has never been rebuilt. There is a khan in the town, appropriated as a deposit and place of safety to merchants and their goods.

Not least among the European travelers to visit Damascus (1502) before the downfall of the Mamlūks was Ludovico di Varthema of Bologna, who admired the citadel:

> You must know that in the said city of Damascus there is a very beautiful and strong castle. . . . And, moreover, in each angle of the said castle the arms of Florence are sculptured in marble. It is surrounded by very wide fosses, and has four extremely strong towers and drawbridges, and powerful and excellent artillery are constantly mounted there. Fifty Mamelukes, in the service of the Grand Sultan, are constantly quartered with the governor of the castle.

Shortly before Varthema was in Damascus, al-Badri, an Egyptian with a keen eye for strongholds and a lasting interest in places of beauty, wrote a book on the traits of Damascus. Of the citadel he said:

> The citadel [of Damascus] is like a town. . . . It has a mosque with khutbah like the city. . . . In it there is a bath, a mill and some shops. The mint is there. Houses and storerooms exist in it also. Its *fārima* [bastille] has no equal on the face of this earth. . . . Tīmūr failed to destroy it completely. . . . The citadel has its water reservoirs and its drainage system. . . . So in times of siege the inhabitants of the citadel would not suffer need.

Other official sites of renown in Damascus included the residence of Baybars, the Hall of Justice, and the many *maydāns* (public squares), of which al-Akhḍar and al-Haṣa were two of the most widely known. The governor's processions and military parades were held in the latter, and there, too, the sultan played *sawalajān* or watched horse races. Maydān Taḥt al-Qal'a boasted of clowns, conjurers, and storytellers, especially on summer nights.

To the south of the city there was a *maydān,* not far from present-day al-Qadam, which, although not frequently used, was a busy place at least twice a year: at the departure of the pilgrims and on their return. Travelers and writers on Damascus never failed to record a description of the impressive occasion. (I remember enjoying such an occasion as a child when my family lived in Damascus.) "One of the strangest things told [to] us," wrote Ibn Jubayr, "is that when the pilgrims from Damascus, together with those from the Maghrib who had joined them, returned to the city in this year of 580 [1184], a vast concourse of people, men and women, went forth to meet them, shaking the hands of the pilgrims and touching them, giving dinars to the poor amongst them that they met, and offering them food." Of the European visitors who were impressed by this festive occasion, Bertrandon de la Brocquiere has left a vivid description of the pilgrims' return:

> On the morrow of my arrival I saw the caravan return from Mecca. It was said to be composed of three thousand camels; and, in fact, it was two days and as many nights before they had all entered the town. This event was, according to custom, a great festival. The governor of Damascus, attended by the principal persons of the town, went to meet the caravan out of respect to the Alcoran, which it bore. This is the book of law which Mohammed left to his followers. It was enveloped in a silken covering, painted over with Moorish inscriptions; and the camel that bore it was, in like manner, decorated all over with silk. Four musicians, and a great number of drums and trumpets, preceded the camel, and made a loud noise. In front, and around, were about thirty men—some bearing cross-bows, others drawn swords, others small harquebuses, which they fired off every now and then. Behind this camel followed eight old men, mounted on the swiftest camels, and near them were led their horses, magnificently caparisoned and ornamented with rich saddles, according to the custom of the country. After them came a Turkish lady, a relation of the grand seignior, in a litter borne by two camels with rich housings. There were many of these animals covered with cloth of gold. The caravan was composed of Moors, Turks, Barbaresques, Tartars, Persians, and other sectaries of the prophet Mohammed.

The public building par excellence in Damascus was, and continued to be, the Great Umayyad Mosque, mainly because, unlike other public buildings, it was not used exclusively by one group or another but was open to every member of the Muslim community. Ibn Batuta, a fourteenth-century Moroccan world traveler who spent some time in Damascus, has given the congregational mosque of Damascus a justifiably long description which, although based on Ibn Jubayr, has a number of personal touches that are a pleasure to read. Ibn Batuta observed that the mosque had thirteen officiating imams. He also noticed that in this mosque "there are a great many 'sojourners' who never leave it, occupying themselves unremittingly in prayer and recitation of the Qur'ān and liturgies, and using for their ablutions those lavatories which are inside the eastern minaret, as we have described above. The townsfolk supply their needs of food and clothing, although the sojourners never beg for anything of the kind from them." Ibn Batuta described teaching in the mosque:

> There are in this mosque several "circles" of instruction in the various branches of [sacred] knowledge, while the traditionists read the Books of Tradition, sitting in high chairs, and the Qur'ān-readers recite in pleasing voices morning and evening. It contains also a number of teachers of the Book of God, each of whom leans his back upon one of the pillars of the mosque, dictating to the children and making them recite, for they abstain from writing down the Qur'ān on their tablets out of reverence for the Book of God [lest it suffer pollution], and so recite it from dictation only. The teacher of writing is a different person from the teacher of the Qu'rān, and he uses books of poetry and the like for teaching them

[the children]. The pupil moves from the class for religious instruction to the writing class, and then becomes expert in calligraphy, because the teacher of writing teaches nothing else.

Al-'Umari's fourteenth-century summary of the functions of the Great Umayyad Mosque is probably one of the best such descriptions still extant. He wrote as follows:

> This mosque is full of people during the day and [the] ends of the night, because people go through it to schools, sūqs and houses. In it one finds more than in any other mosque imāmas, readers [of the Koran], shaykhs of knowledge and teaching, leaders of fatwa and people learned in the Ḥadith [traditions], besides mujāwirīn [dwellers in the mosque] and pious men. Its times are always full with goodness and prayers. One hardly sees it without a worshipper, a meditator, a chanter of the Qur'ān, a mu'adhdhin [caller to prayer], a reader in a book of science, an enquirer about a religious matter, an expositor of a sectarian opinion, or a seeker for a solution of a problem. Some people come in search of a chat, others to meet friends, or to stroll in its court, enjoying the beauties of the moon and stars. The spacious court, the fresh air and the coolness of its passages in time of excessive heat are all attractive to the people.

The markets and merchandise of Damascus have always given visitors coming from the east, south, and north a great deal of delight. The Damascus of the Mamlūks was no exception, and neither were its European visitors. Some observed not only of the type of goods sold but also the organization of trades. Others have supplied information concerning the organization of labor.

Syria is a wealthy country, and her position on trade routes was a decided advantage in the Middle Ages. Damascus benefited not only from such trade but from local industries, especially crafts, as well. Damascus produced sugar and nuts and manufactured cotton and silk textiles, glassware, porcelain, pottery, metalwork, paper, soap, perfumes, flower and rose water, candles, and shoes. The city was also well known for its silver work and goldsmiths. Damascus was favorably compared with Cairo and was considered by some Europeans to be superior to Paris and Florence.

Our guides to the major business districts of Damascus during the fourteenth and fifteenth centuries are a few European travelers whose visits to the Holy Land, such as those of Niccolo of Poggibonsi, Lionardo Frescobaldi, Giorgio Gucci, Simone Sigoli, and Von Suchem, or to the Middle East and the Orient, such as the journeys of Bertrandon de la Brocquiere and Ludovico di Varthema, led them to Damascus. We shall accompany them throughout their walks in various parts of the city. Their stories, woven together, form a colorful tapestry of Damascene markets and merchandise.

> Within the city walls all streets were well covered over with many hanging lamps to light the night; and the houses were very high, made of wood, which did not appear, the interiors being all covered with a light blue, and the floors of mosaic; and few were the houses which did not have their own sculptured fountains, which were marvels to see.
>
> Although about twenty thousand people would leave for Mecca, it did not appear that a person had left, and many streets were [as] full of people as they would be in Florence

on the day of St. John. As the city was full of people, so it was full of merchants and artisans, and each art had its own shops apart in different parts of the city.

In Damascus, more work of whatever kind, of little or great value, was done than in any other part of the world, in silk cloth, cotton cloth, linen cloth, gold and silver work, copper and brass work of every description, and every kind of glass. In that place they excelled in all these, and very great masters they were in every art. Then they had almost every kind of very good fruit, and they preserved it all from one year to another. Then there was always snow in Damascus; and in summer they put it on the [various kinds of] fruit, so they were fresh when eaten, and so iced were they that it was a pleasure [to eat them]. In Damascus all foods were sold on the street, [such] as bread, water, cooked meat of every kind, and every sort of fruit, since the people over there did no cooking at home. But they sent out for everything they wanted, and throughout the whole city there were in several places cooks, with a great deal of every kind of meat; and they made kitchen in everything, and they cooked well and clean: and so they gave to others any kind of meat or kitchen a man might wish, and the amount a man might want, and so they went through the city selling the said things. And those who went about selling their things carried a table on four legs on their heads; and on it was a fire-place with a pan, all the while aboiling; with meat, a bowl, a small ladle, the water and the salt and everything necessary. And the people set [*sic*] themselves down on benches on the street to eat; and he [who sold the food] would wait until they had eaten; and they drank mere water, or certain waters with dried grapes or prepared some other way, and they spent little on their food, on their kitchen, or on their dress.

Now as to the merchandise of Damascus; this would be incredible to him who had not seen with his own eyes, because so very great was the number of merchants and artisans through the whole city, within and without. In the suburbs there was not a span of ground to ask for or imagine: the most beautiful things in the world were found there, of the noblest and richest work, so that going asightseeing, there are such rich and noble and delicate works of every kind that if you had money in the bone of your leg, without fail you would break it to buy of these things, because you know not to imagine with the mind that kind of thing that was not found here, whichever way it was made. Here was found a great deal of silk cloth of every kind and colour, the most beautiful and best in the world. Here also was found a very great deal of cotton [fabrics], of the world's most beautiful, so that if one saw the finest, and he were not a perfect connoisseur, he would believe they were silk, so very fine and bright and delicate and beautiful were they. Brocades were also available in the markets. Here also was made a great deal of brass basins and pitchers, and really they appeared of gold, and then on the said basins and pitchers were made figures and foliage and other fine work in silver, so that it was a very beautiful thing to see.

And so of all the trades there were the most perfect and great masters, and truly the order they had among them was a beautiful and noble thing, for if the father was a goldsmith, the sons could not ever have a trade other than this, and so they went from generation to generation, so that of necessity they must be perfect masters of their arts. Then their shops were so well ordered and were kept so neat and clean that they were a pleasure to see, and they were all full of merchandise and packed; and the more they sold, the sooner they were refurnished, because they had stores, and the houses where they dwelt were full of merchandise.

Really to write of the great multitude of merchandise which was in Damascus would be a confusion to the would-be writer, and still a greater confusion to him who did not see. And yet wishing to make mention of how many were the trades and kinds of things, it would be too long to narrate. For in addition to what has been said, the sūqs of Damascus had precious stones, jewels and spices that came from India. It was said by the Christians who were acquainted that really all Christendom could be supplied for a year with the merchandise of Damascus. Now, imagine what a noble thing this must be when seen with the eye: [the] tongue cannot say, neither can the mind imagine.

In the said city there lived a very great number of people, so that the streets and ways of Damascus were ever packed with people. There was a fine order which they had in guarding by night the streets of the merchants and the artisans. The greater part of the streets of Damascus were covered with roofs or vaulted, with openings that admit light enough when needed, and when night came they lighted many glass lamps in every street, and from one lamp to the other was twelve braccia, and the light of night was seen like that of day, so many were the lamps they lighted. They said that more than thirty thousand lamps were lighted every evening in all the streets, and in every street there were watchmen to guard the shops, and nobody dared go about at night without a lamp in hand, and if one was perhaps found without a light, he would be taken and led before the admiral, and he would pay the fixed fine. And so in this way no harm was ever done. Again having regard to the great number of people dwelling in that city, one would say they had always the best market

> of bread, of every kind of meat, and the best things, save wine, because the inhabitants drank no wine. Also there was a great scarcity of firewood. They sold everything by weight. Due to this lack of wood many citizens did not cook at home, nay, there was a great number of cooks as clean as ermine, and one could have, clean and good, whatever you wished cooked.

Bertrandon de la Brocquiere was in Damascus about the middle of the fifteenth century, arriving there from Beirut. After a visit to northern Palestine, he traveled even farther north. After agreeing to join the retinue of a Mamlūk who was going to Turkey, he purchased the things he needed. His personal experiences and his observations on Damascus are reproduced here in full.

> I went immediately after this interview, with one of my friends, to the market, called the Bazaar, and bought two long white robes that reached to my ancles [*sic*], a complete turban, a linen girdle, a fustian pair of drawers to tuck the ends of my robe in; two small bags, the one for my own use the other to hang on my horse's head while feeding him with barley and straw; a leathern spoon and salt; a carpet to sleep on; and, lastly, a paletot of white skin, which I lined with linen cloth, and which was of service to me in the nights. I purchased also a white tarquais [a type of quiver] complete to which hung a sword and knives; but as to the tarquais and sword, I could only buy them privately; for if those who have the administration of justice had known of it, the seller and myself would have run great risks.
>
> The Damascus blades are the handsomest and best of all Syria; and it is curious to observe their manner of burnishing them. This operation, is performed before tempering; and they have, for this purpose, a small piece of wood, in which

is fixed an iron, which they rub up and down the blade, and thus clear off all inequalities, as a plane does to wood. They then temper and polish it. This polish is so highly finished, that, when any one wants to arrange his turban, he uses his sword for a looking-glass. As to its temper, it is perfect; and I have nowhere seen swords that cut so excellently. There are made at Damascus, and in the adjoining country, mirrors of steel, that magnify objects like burning glasses. I have seen some that, when exposed to the sun, have reflected the heat so strongly as to set fire to a plank fifteen or sixteen feet distant.

Damascus may contain, as I have heard, one hundred thousand souls. The town is rich, commercial, and, after Cairo, the most considerable of all in the possession of the sultan. To the north, south, and east is an extensive plain; to the west rises a mountain, at the foot of which the suburbs are built. A river runs through it, which is divided into several canals. The town only is inclosed by a handsome wall, for the suburbs are larger than the town. I have nowhere seen such extensive gardens, better fruits, nor greater plenty of water. This is said to be so abundant, that there is scarcely a house without a fountain. The governor is only inferior to the sultan in all Syria and Egypt; but, as at different times some governors have revolted, the sultans have taken precautions to restrain them within proper bounds.

·4·

Damascus and Suburbs

SUBURBAN DAMASCUS developed under new conditions: economic prosperity, the rule of law, the reconquest of coastal areas from the Crusaders, and more concentration on Syrian trade routes because of difficulties along the northern trade routes, which passed through Byzantine lands. Many a visitor to the city in the fourteenth and fifteenth centuries noted that the Damascus outside the walls was larger than the walled Damascus.

Ibn Batuta, to whom the suburbs were of particular interest, mentions those which Ibn Jubayr had seen—al-Nayrab, al-Mizzah, and Qāsyūn—and, in addition, gives us a description of al-Rabwa and al-Ṣāliḥīyah. To him, al-Rabwa, according to tradition and legend, was "the blessed Hill which is mentioned in the Qur'ān." Ibn Batuta was repeating Ibn Jubayr when he said:

> This hill overlooks the gardens which surround the city, and in beauty and extent of the prospect offered to the eyes may boast of a view which no other hill possesses, with these seven streams flowing away in diverse directions, so that the vision

> is dazzled by the charm of their junction and separation, their swift current and their gliding [across the plain]. But the elegance and perfect beauty of al-Rabwa are too great for any description to be adequate. It possesses many endowments of fields, orchards and immovable property, from which are met its expenses for [the stipends of] the imam and the muezzin and [the needs of] travelers.

To this, however, he added his own remarks:

> At the far [west] end of Jabal Qāsyūn is the blessed Hill [al-Rabwa] which is mentioned in the Qur'ān, "furnished with security and a flowing spring," the refuge of Jesus the Messiah and his Mother (on them be peace). It is one of the most beautiful sights in the world and most pleasant of its resorts, and on it are lofty places, noble buildings, and choice gardens. The blessed Refuge is a small cave in the middle part of the hill, of the size of a small room, and opposite it is a one-room building which is said to have been the place of prayer of al-Khiḍr (on him be peace). The people press forward eagerly to make a prayer in his hut. The Refuge has a small iron door, and is encircled by the mosque; the latter has circular ambulatories and a beautiful fountain to which the water comes down from above. It is led through a channel in the wall, which connects with a marble tank, into which the water falls. There is nothing to compare with it in beauty and strangeness of shape. Nearby are lavatories for the ceremonial ablutions, supplied with running water.

As a result of the prolonged Crusader occupation of Jerusalem (1099), some pious Muslims decided to emigrate from the Holy City to escape domination by the Christians. One such man was Abū 'Umar Ibn Qudāma al-Maqdisī (the

Jerusalemite), who emigrated to Damascus with a fairly large following which became even larger with time. Al-Maqdisī and his followers first settled at the Mosque of Abū Ṣāliḥ, outside the East Gate. Later they moved to the flank of Mount Qāsyūn, where they established a *madrasah* (theological seminary) and convent for the Ḥanbalites. In their new location they were referred to as *al-Ṣāliḥīn,* meaning "the good people," or more probably because of their earlier association with the Mosque of Abū Ṣāliḥ. In either event, the new suburb came to be known as al-Ṣāliḥīyah, after them.

Ibn Batuta says of al-Ṣāliḥīyah, which was flourishing at the time of his visit:

> Damascus is surrounded on all sides except the east by suburbs of extensive area, the interiors of which are pleasanter than the interior of Damascus itself, owing to the narrowness which characterizes its lanes. To the north of the city is the suburb of al-Ṣāliḥīyah, a great city [in itself], with a bazaar of unparalleled beauty, and containing a congregational mosque and a hospital. There is a college there, known as the college of Ibn 'Umar, which is endowed for the benefit of aged men and men of mature age who desire to learn the holy Qu'rān, to whom, and to those who teach them, there is a regular issue of food and clothing sufficient for their needs. In Damascus there is a college of the same kind, known as the college of Ibn Munajjā. The inhabitants of al-Ṣāliḥīyah all adhere to the school of the imam Aḥmad Ibn Ḥanbal (God be pleased with him).

By the end of the period discussed here, al-Ṣāliḥīyah had seven *dārs* (special houses) for *ḥadīths,* sixteen *ribāṭs* (garrisoned barracks), thirty-eight *ḥārahs,* and seventy-one mosques.

A later writer enumerated some of the fruits and vegetables which al-Ṣāliḥīyah and other suburban gardens of Damascus produced. These included apples, plums, mulberries, pomegranates, figs, lettuce, and asparagus. Flowers, especially lilies and violets, were also raised.

With the exception of its eastern flank, then, Damascus was surrounded by flourishing suburbs with homes, schools, mosques, markets, and places of attraction. And the last-named were not lacking around Damascus, which seems to have been favored by nature. With the Ghūṭah, al-Jabha, Wādi al-Banafsaj, Bayn al-Nahrayn, Qaṭya, and al-Yalakī near by, Damascenes had field for choice of where to spend a pleasant day in spring, summer, or autumn. Every one of these places had shops which sold cooked food and sweets, and there were shelters for any and all who might need them. Devout persons could even go to a *zāwiya,* where they could join others in religious rites and practices. Some went to the precincts of Christian monasteries for the joys of the day, and they were almost always well received. Generally speaking, however, people spent their leisure time picnicking—and they behaved themselves. Those who sought interests and activities that were not acceptable to the community betook themselves to more secluded places, which were not completely lacking.

* * *

A number of references have been made to schools in Damascus; it seems appropriate to discuss them more fully at this point in our study.

It has been possible to secure the names of eighty-six schools existing in Damascus under the Mamlūks, some of which had been established before their rule. Two of them were medical schools and were attached to the *bīmāristāns;* the others were schools for religious instruction, which was limited to three of the four Sunnite rites: Shāfi'i, Ḥanafi and Ḥanbali. The Malikites were not prominent in the Syria of the Mamlūks, but occasional references to a few Malikite schools are to be found in various works dealing with that period.

Of the 84 religious schools in Mamlūk Damascus, 35 were Shāfi'ite, 34 Ḥanafite, 8 Ḥanbalite, and 7 were "common," that is, common to more than one rite. It should be noted that the Ayyūbids were Shāfi'ites and that Damascus had always had only a Shāfi'ite chief justice until Baybars decreed that Cairo, Damascus, and Aleppo should each have four chief justices. The Ḥanbalites had only recently established themselves as a strong group in Damascus, having migrated from the East, principally Baghdad, in the late eleventh and early twelfth centuries.

Schools were well provided for. The practice of establishing an endowment to provide the needs of an institution is old in Islam, and the process seems to have been enhanced during the sovereignty of the Saljūqs, Zangids, Ayyūbids, and Mamlūks. Rulers set the pace, and wealthy people followed the good example. Usually, a *waqf*—a charitable endowment—for a *madrasah* provided teachers, who sometimes numbered as many as thirty, with water, light, and furniture. Some larger bequests even secured bread and money for the students. One often finds mention of schools whose funds were the income of a *sūq,* a few gardens, a bath, and one or two other business ventures. Al-Madrasah al-Rīḥānīya had a *waqf* of two orchards, a tract of land, two vegetable gardens, five-sixths of a farm, and a stable. In the case of another school, al-Juwānīya, we may cite its expenditures as testimony to a generous endowment. Each of its teachers, and there were approximately 25 of them, received 130 dirhams ($9.10) and one large measure of wheat and another of barley (for his beast of burden) per month; the nazir, or superintendent, received 10 per cent of the school's income for his toil, attention, and supervision of its property; and 800 dirhams ($56.00) were to be spent annually for the celebration of the Feast of Sha'bān. The nazir could, if he saw fit, increase the number of teachers and other appointees.

The buildings which housed these schools were enormous and beautiful: the Mamlūks built genuine edifices of learning. A courtyard, with a sculptured marble fountain in the center, was surrounded on four sides by colonnaded cloisters, one of which opened into a mosque on one side, while a second opened into a vast chamber, with a dome, in which was often to be seen the tomb of the builder, on another side. The third and fourth cloisters opened to rooms used for reading and instruction.

Each school had its own nazir, whose duties included the supervision and administration of its *waqf,* the keeping of its accounts, and the spending of its income according to the stipulations of its endowment. The nazir was always a learned man, often *qāḍi al-quḍat* (chief justice) of the rite, and another of his duties was to teach. The staff included *muḥaddithīn* (traditionalists), *qārīs* (readers of the Qur'ān), *faqīhs* (jurists), and *shaikh al-naḥw* (masters of Arabic grammar).

In one or two schools in Damascus, instruction in arithmetic and logic was known to have been given.

Suburban schools were often very large. Such were those of al-Ṣāliḥīyah—al-Ḍiyā'īya, al-Atābikiya, al-Ṣāḥiba, and al-'Umarīya. And they were richly endowed. Al-Ḍiyā'īya had a library which contained, according to Ibn 'Abdul Hādī, even the Old and the New Testaments; it continued under good stewardship until Tīmūr's attack on Damascus. Al-'Umarīya was probably the most influential of al-Ṣāliḥīyah's schools. Founded by 'Umar Ibn Qudāma, himself a great *'ālim* (religious teacher), late in the twelfth century as a Ḥanbalite school, it was converted into a school for all Sunnites. Gradually, as new wings and buildings were added, it became a complex of halls, courts, a mosque, and small rooms where students could live. It was so richly endowed that its superintendent gave away one thousand loaves of bread daily, in addition to the bread rations given to members of the teaching staff. During Ramaḍān, the month of fasting for Muslims, hundreds of people received their evening meal from its kitchen: meat, cereals, and desert. On the occasions of the feasts, richer foods and sweets were served to those present, and other benefits, such as the use of utensils and hot water, were extended. Al-'Umarīya's library was exceptionally rich, and its use was not restricted to occupants only.

* * *

Between 1150 and 1500, Damascus received six *bīmāristāns,* or hospitals, of which two were extant when Ibn Jubayr visited the city in 1184. The *bīmāristān* of Nūr al-Dīn, known as al-Nūrī, was enlarged in the thirteenth century and continued to impress visitors and historians well into the fifteenth. Other *bīmāristāns* were built near Bāb al-Barīd, in the central *maydān,* in al-Ṣāliḥīyah, and at al-Nayrab.

Essentially, a *bīmāristān* was built by the ruler, but at least two of Damascus' six hospitals were erected by individuals. Founders of *bīmāristāns,* like builders of schools, saw to it that enough income was secured for their maintenance; large *waqfs* were usually left for these institutions. Al-Bīmāristān al-Qaymarī, at al-Ṣāliḥīyah, received the income of two villages, parts of other places amounting to two and one-half villages, certain areas with water mills, thirty-five shops, a stable, two khans, and some other property.

Most *bīmāristāns* were divided into two sections, one for men and the other for women. There were wards for surgery, internal diseases, and diseases of the eye; lunatics had their own wards. All wards were supervised by specialists; they, in turn, reported to the nazir, whose appointment was made only after much deliberation. On the occasion of his appointment, a nazir received instructions and injunctions as to how to deal with patients. Nor did the nazir of a *bīmāristān* need be a physician himself: the job was considered to be one requiring administrative ability and conscientious attention rather than medical acumen.

Al-Bīmāristān al-Qaymarī was founded by a Mamlūk amir of Kurdish origin, Sayf al-Dīn (d.1257) by name. It was situated on the slope of the mountain, with Damascus and the city's orchards just below; even Tīmūr is said to have enjoyed the view. It consisted of one large hall supported by piers, on both sides of which stood two smaller halls, for patients. Adjoining these were two spacious chambers (one for men, the other for women) for people suffering from dysentery and diarrhea. A large room was used to store medicines of all sorts. An out-patient clinic was open on Mondays and Thursdays; free medication was given to all patients. The hospital's kitchen prepared both ordinary and dietary meals. A special section for the insane completed the complex arrangement. Al-Bīmāristān al-Qaymarī's staff included a physician, an oculist, a chemist, and a host of male and female nurses and servants; a nazir supervised the place and administered its affairs. The table below shows its personnel and their remunerations.

Staff Member(s)	*Individual Monthly Salary (in Dirhams)*	*(In Measures of Wheat) Monthly Rations*
Physicians (3)	60–70	½ to 1
Superintendent	40	½
Oculist	45	½
Male servants (3)	13	⅙
Female attendants	10	⅙
Pharmacist	26	⅓
Chief superintendent of the *waqf*	60	1 and 1 barley
Imam	40	⅓
Mason	13	⅙
Porters	8	⅙

Some hospitals had medical schools attached to them. One such *bīmāristān* was al-Nūrī, where physicians attended to the patients and lectured on medicine in a house adjoining the *bīmāristān*. The courses and lectures in medicine enjoyed a great deal of freedom, for they were not subject to government control. The teachers and physicians at al-Nūrī produced thirty-six books on various aspects of medicine—quite voluminous for one institution!

One of the most prominent physicians and teachers of medicine of the period was Ibn 'Ali al-Dakhwār, who also taught medicine at his home. When he died, he left his house to be used as a medical school, with an endowment large enough to provide for the teacher and his assistants.

It is rather safe to conclude that insofar as medical knowledge was of social value and its advancement was a social force in the life of the city and the country, the *bīmāristān* and its medical school, unhampered by convention or legalism, were centers of this advancement.

* * *

Our tour of Damascus—its citadel, mosque, *maydāns, sūqs,* suburbs, schools, and *bīmāristāns*—cannot be complete without a visit to its *zāwiyas.*

When the Islamic state expanded into many territories, its distant parts, as well as parts which were exposed to internal rebellious movements, needed constant vigil. Gradually, *ribāṭs,* or garrisoned barracks, were developed; in them lived defenders of the faith and the state, who kept watch over frontiers or weak points. These *ribāṭs,* when situated in cities or towns, later served also as meeting places for the followers of one Sufi order or another. As the Sufis gradually became more organized from the eleventh century on, they had their own meeting places, which were called *khānqās* or *zāwiyas,* the former being of Persian origin and the latter of Arabic. A *zāwiya* implied, in more cases than one, a place where religious people lived. By the thirteenth century, however, the three words—*ribāṭ, khānqā,* and *zāwiya*—had come to be used without differentiation, and their uses had become almost identical. Damascus was no exception.

According to various authorities, during the reign of the Mamlūks, Damascus had seventy-eight of these convents for men and two for women. Their inhabitants, whether natives or foreigners, whether permanent or transient, had nothing to worry about—they were amply provided for. They could therefore devote their time to religious practices and learning, for the *zāwiyas* were centers for education in almost the same way schools were, except that they were more limited, even in the religious fields. It must be remembered that in Islam, education and the manifestation of piety could not be easily separated.

We have already seen what Ibn Jubayr had to say generally about the *zāwiyas*. We accompany him once more on a visit to another of them, probably one of the most magnificent Damascus ever knew:

> One of their most splendid convents is a place called al-Qasr [the Palace], an enormous structure rising alone into the skies. In its upper story are apartments than which I have never seen more beautiful for their lofty site. It is half a mile distant from the city, and has an extensive garden connected with it. It had once been a pleasure lodge of a Turk. . . . Nūr al-Dīn demanded it from the owner as a gift, and then gave it in perpetual endowment to the Sufis.

Under the Mamlūks, Damascus, like many other places, enjoyed the presence of many of the more widely known Sufi orders which throve in the world of Islam. Of these, al-Qādirīya, al-Rifā'īya, al-Wafā'īya, al-Qalandarīya, and al-Nubuwīya were probably the most prominent and, comparatively speaking, commanded large followings in Damascus.

The *zāwiya* of Ibn Dāwūd was the biggest in al-Ṣāliḥīyah. It had water reservoirs, a huge court, a beautifully built mosque, numerous rooms for the poor, a library, and a special quarter for women. It had its own teachers and preachers, and people assembled there every Tuesday evening for Sufi *dhikr* (singing of liturgies).

·5·

People and Problems

Medieval visitors to Damascus ranked it second only to Cairo in size, and Europeans frequently said that it had more people than either Paris or Florence. Estimates of the number of its inhabitants varied, but it can be safely assumed that about 100,000 people were living there.

The residents of the city were primarily Arabs, who used Arabic at home, at school, and in the market place, but under the Mamlūks, non-Arabic-speaking groups had come to settle there or were brought in by the authorities. Turkmen had arrived with the Zangids, if not earlier; Saladin brought Kurds with him; Circassian and Turkish soldiers were companions of Mamlūk governors and officers.

Most of the people were Muslims, but Christians and Jews also lived in Damascus. The Christians lived in their own quarter in the southeastern part of the city near Bāb Tūma (St. Thomas Gate), and the Jews lived in a similar section in the same part of the city south of the Street Called Straight, which ran from Jābiya Gate to East Gate. Benjamin of Tudela estimated the Jewish population in Damascus at three thousand, "many of whom are learned and rich men." He also mentions two hundred Samaritans. I have not found estimates of the number of native Christians, but I am inclined to believe that they were more numerous than the Jews.

Ibn Jubayr says of the Damascus cathedral:

> Inside the city is a church held in great consideration by the Rūm [Christians]. It is called St. Mary's Church, and after the one in Jerusalem they have none more esteemed than this. It is an elegant structure with remarkable pictures that amaze the mind and hold the gaze, and its spectacle is wonderful indeed. It is in the hands of the Rūm, who are never molested within it.

A European traveler visiting Damascus in the fourteenth century described the places revered by Christians as follows:

> Then on the IX day of the said month, about noon, we were in Damascus: which is a large and beautiful city of notable and marvelous things, and in almost everything excels all the others subject to the Sultan; and to say Damascus for them is like saying Paris for us. First, half a mile from Damascus is where Christ struck St. Paul, saying: Saule, Saule, cur me persequeris? Then there is also on the wall of Damascus a window whence he fled when the Jews had taken him and placed him in prison; and then St. Paul went to Jerusalem to find St. Peter. And there is in the said Damascus the house of Ananias, to whom God told St. Paul to go, when He struck him as already related, and Ananias baptized him. And about two stone's throws from the wall of Damascus there is a field where the majority of the Christians are buried, who in that city die, be they our Christians or Greeks or Armenians or Christians of the Girdle; and in the middle of this field and

these tombs there is a square stone, more than a braccio on every side, and it is a stone of white marble and it is said that it was on that stone that St. George was beheaded. And all the Christians over there have great devotion for this place, and they go there every day, and especially on Christian feast days, so that it is like a consecration to kiss the stone: and all the pilgrims take a little of it. And it is said that Job was born in the said city of Damascus, on a slope V miles from Damascus and visible from every part of Damascus, and likewise near the road outside Damascus there is a field where, they say, Cain killed Abel.

Then about XII miles from Damascus there is a devout and beautiful church, and a monastery; and this is a monastery of Christian Greek women: and in all this voyage in those parts we found no other monastery of women. And the church and the monastery are devout and beautiful, and in many things like ours here: and the roof and the covering are of tiles, and the Christians and the Saracens have great devotion for it. And in times past for the oppression by the Christians of the Saracens, now in one way, now in another the Saracens of those parts have oppressed the Christians, even the religious; but ever they held this place in such veneration that they never did to it anything novel. True it is said that a certain great Saracen of the country, who was at one time an official in the country, had wished to oppress this monastery; and God suddenly showed manifest miracles by blinding them [the Saracens] and taking from them the use of their hands and like things, and they did not regain them until they had ceased from doing evil. Then there is an icon of Our Lady for which there is great devotion in the said place, and it is said that twice it was furtively and in secret taken from the said place and taken to Jerusalem and every time of itself it returned to the said monastery: and there emanates from the said icon a certain oil which the said Sisters give to the pilgrims for which there is great devotion. The said place is in a beautiful fruitful country; and we stopped there a night and half a day: and then we returned to Damascus.

There was a small European colony in Damascus in the fourteenth and fifteenth centuries, composed essentially of business people—Venetians, Catalans, Genoese, Florentines, Calabrians, and Frenchmen—and according to some travelers they were numerous. They had many warehouses in the city, warehouses which contained various cloths, silk and satin, velvets, brass, and all other merchandise that was salable. Many merchants were especially interested in purchasing spiceries, which they shipped to Europe via Beirut. They had consuls or bailiffs to look after their affairs; at least we know of the existence of a consul for the Catalans and a bailiff for the Venetians. These people, or some distinguished merchant, would act as hosts to important European visitors coming to Damascus.

Native Christians and Jews in Damascus, as in all Islamic states, were considered *dhimmis,* which means "protected people of the Book." They paid a poll tax and were deprived of the duties of citizens. The protections, prescribed in the Qur'ān and the Ahadith and adhered to by many caliphs and responsible people very often, did not always provide the necessary guarantees. Under the Mamlūks—and they were no exception—people were subjected to confiscation of property, forced contributions to the state or sultan, and maltreatment for various reasons. Christians and Jews were constantly exposed to this sort of thing; but sometimes Muslims received a similar treatment.

Foreign Christians often fared better at the hands of the state if they were protected by treaties, but the populace did not always feel bound to accept this. Hence there are reports of occasional rough handling of visitors by youngsters, who often managed to escape the watchful eyes of state officials. Apparently, one way in which the government tried to afford protection to foreign Christian merchants was to compel them to remain in their homes at night. Bertrandon de la Brocquiere says of this: "Every evening the [Christian] merchants are shut up in their houses by persons appointed for this purpose, who, on the morrow, come to open their gates, when it may please them."

* * *

Damascenes have always been known for their courteous behavior, both among themselves and toward strangers. Their kindness and interest in other people impressed numerous sojourners. The observations of Ibn Jubayr and Ibn Batuta, both of whom hailed from the western part of the Muslim world (and the latter had traveled extensively in more distant lands and seas), are worthy of being quoted in full. Ibn Jubayr writes:

> The people of these parts address each other as Mulai [Lord] and Sayyid [Sir], and use the expressions "Your Servant" and "Your Excellency." When one meets another, instead of giving the ordinary greeting he says respectfully, "Here is your slave," or "Here is your servant at your service."

They make presents of honorifics to each other. Gravity with them is a fabulous affair.

Their style of salutation is either a deep bow or a prostration, and you will see their necks at play, lifting and lowering, stretching and contracting. Sometimes they will go on like this for a long time, one going down as the other rises, their turbans tumbling between them. This style of greeting, inclining as in prayer, we have observed in female slaves, or when handmaids make some request. How strange are these men! How can they assume the manners of anklet-wearers [women]? They apply themselves with assiduity to things that proud souls disdain, and practice abuses of the capitation, which Muslim law forbids. In this direction they have many vain customs. What odd people! If they treat each other in this way, reaching such an extravagance of epithets in their common intercourse, how do they address their sultans and comport themselves with such? The tail is equal to the head with them, and they do not distinguish between the governor and the governed. Glory to God, Who created men of all kinds. He has no partner. There is no God but He.

A singular habit in all these lands is their walking, great and small, with their hands behind their backs, one hand holding the other. They make their deep inclinations of greeting in this fashion, which has an air of obedience in token of humbleness and modesty, as if they had been treated with violence, and had had their hands bound behind their backs. They deem this posture to set them apart as persons of distinction and honour, as well as giving liveliness to their limbs and relief from fatigue. The venerable among them is he who draws his train a span along the ground, or puts his hands behind his back, one over the other. They have adopted this manner of walking as obligatory, and every one of them has embellished himself with this practice and seen it to be good. I beg the pardon of God for them.

But in the etiquette of shaking hands they have usages which renew their security [with God] and invite God's pardon [for their other faults], according to the preaching of the tradition transmitted from the Prophet of God—may God bless and preserve him—on the matter of hand-shaking. They employ them after the prayers, more especially after the morning and afternoon prayers. When the imām salutes [the congregation] and has ended the prayers, the people go to him and shake his hand and then advance on each other, shaking hands with those to right and left of them. They then leave this pardon-bringing service with the grace of Great and Glorious God. We have already mentioned in this narrative how they employ this habit of shaking each other's hands when they observe the new moon, and how they pray for each other the blessings and happiness of the new month, and that they might be accompanied by felicity and well-being during that month and those that will follow. That also is a beneficial practice, for which God will advantage them because of the prayers for each other, the renewal of affection, and the shaking of each other's hands by the Faithful. [All of this is from] the mercy and favour of God Most High.

Of people's interest in endowments and the care of strangers, Ibn Jubayr had this to say:

To this hill [near Bait Laḥya] are attached many pious endowments, comprising gardens, arable lands, and houses [whose revenues] are assigned to their various uses. Some are allotted under the heading of expenses for the subsistence of visitors who stay there, some for clothing under the heading of covering for the night, and some for food. There are allocations to cover all needs, including those of the resident guardian as imām and the muezzin charged with the service of the place, who draw a fixed monthly stipend from this source. It is a great institution. The present guardian is one of the murābiṭs [Marabouts, or monks] from Massuf and one of their chief men, called Abu'l Rabī' Sulayman ibn Ibrāhīm ibn Mālik, who has standing with the sultan and the leading personages of the realm. He receives five dinārs monthly, exclusive of the revenue of the hill. Kindness is impressed on his features and stamped on him. He is an incumbent of one of those benefices that provide Maghrib strangers lonely in these lands with means of support, such as an imamate in a mosque, lodgement in a school with expenses paid, an appointment to a zāwiya in a congregational mosque and gaining a livelihood there, assisting in the sectional reading of the seven parts of the Koran, or the curatorship of a blessed shrine and receiving a benefice from its endowments and such like ways of living of the same blessed pattern as would take long to describe; and the needy stranger, so long as he has come for righteous purposes, will be cared for without being given cause to blush. The other strangers who are not in this state and who have a trade or craft, are also found divers means of livelihood, such as being a watchman in a garden, supervisor of a bath, or keeper of the clothes of the bathers, manager of a mill, custodian of boys, conducting them to school and returning them to their homes, and many other occupations. In all this they trust only strangers from the Maghrib, for their fame for honesty is high and their repute has spread. The people of the town do not trust their own fellow citizens. This is one of the gifts of God Most High towards strangers. Praise and thanks to Him for what He has granted to His servants.

Should one of the holders of these benefices wish to have audience of the Sultan, the ruler will receive him and treat him liberally, granting him a salary paid according to his ability and office. These virtues are part of the natural character of these people and their king, both of old and now. The discussion has led us successively to another question than that which we were on, but the excursus was needful. God is the guarantor of real help. There is no Lord but He.

The conveniences for strangers in this city are beyond computation, more especially for those who commit to memory the Book of Great and Glorious God and those devoted to study, to whom the attitude of this town is most extraordinary. All these eastern cities are of this fashion, but this city is more populous and wealthy. Whoever of the young men of the Maghrib seeks prosperity, let him move to these lands and leave his country in the pursuit of knowledge and he will find many forms of help. The first of these is the release of the mind from the consideration of livelihood, and this is the greatest and most important. For when zeal is present the student will find the way clear to exert his utmost endeavour, and there will be no excuse for lagging behind, save in the case of those addicted to idleness and procrastination, and to them this exhortation is not addressed. We speak only to the zealous, who in their own land find that the search for the means of living comes between them and their aim of seeking knowledge. Well, then, the door of this East is open, so enter it in peace, industrious youth, and seize the chance of undistracted [study] and seclusion before a wife and children cling to you and you gnash your teeth in regret at the time you have lost. God is the Helper and the Guide. There is no God but He. I have given counsel to those I found listening, and called to those I heard answering. He who is directed by God is on the right path. Glorious is His power. Exalted is His majesty.

If in all these eastern lands there were nothing but the readiness of its people to show bounty to strangers and generosity to the poor, especially in the case of the inhabitants of the countryside [it would be enough]. For you will find admirable their eagerness to show kindness to guests, which is enough to bring them honour. It sometimes comes to pass that one of them offers his piece [of bread] to a poor man, upon whom refusing he will cry and say, "Had God seen in me any good, this needy man would have eaten my food." In this they reveal a noble heart. One of their admirable traits is their respect for the pilgrim, despite the shortness of the distance to Mecca and the ease and facility with which they could make the journey. When the pilgrims return, they stroke them with their hands and press upon them to secure their benedictions.

Ibn Batuta touching on the same subjects, but with more emphasis on the *waqf* aspects, writes:

The varieties of the endowments at Damascus and their expenditure are beyond computation, so numerous are they. There are endowments in aid of persons who cannot undertake the Pilgrimage, out of which are paid to those who go in their stead sums sufficient for their needs. There are endowments for supplying wedding outfits to girls, to those namely whose families are unable to provide them [with the customary paraphernalia]. There are endowments for the freeing of prisoners, and endowments for travellers, out of which they are given food, clothing, and the expenses of conveyance to their countries. There are endowments for the improvement and paving of the streets, because the lanes in Damascus all have a pavement [sidewalk] on either side on which the foot passengers walk, while riders use the roadway in between. Besides these there are endowments for other charitable purposes.

As I went one day along a lane in Damascus, I saw in it a young slave-boy out of whose hand there had just fallen a Chinese porcelain dish (which they call by the name of *ṣaḥn* ["platter"]) and [it] had broken to bits. A crowd gathered round him and one of them said to him, "Pick up the pieces, and take them with you to the custodian of the endowments for utensils." So he picked them up, and the man went with him to the custodian, to whom the slave showed the broken pieces and thereupon received from him enough to buy a similar platter. This endowment is one of the best of good works, for the boy's master would undoubtedly have beaten him for breaking the dish, or at least have scolded him, while he too would have been heartbroken and upset because of that. The benefaction is thus indeed a mender of hearts—may God well reward him whose charitable zeal rose to the height of such an action.

The people of Damascus vie with one another in the building and endowment of mosques, religious houses, colleges, and sanctuaries. They have a high opinion of the Moors of North Africa and freely entrust them with the care of their moneys, wives and children. Every man [of them] who comes to the end of his resources in any district of Damascus finds without exception some means of livelihood opened to him, either as imām in a mosque, or as a reciter in a college, or by occupation of [a cell in] a mosque, where his daily requirements are supplied to him, or by recitation of the Qur'ān, or employment as a keeper at one of the blessed sanctuaries, or else he may be included in the company of Ṣūfis who live in the convents, in receipt of a regular allowance of upkeep-money and clothing. Anyone who is a stranger there living on charity is always protected from [having to earn it at] the expense of his self-respect, and carefully sheltered from anything that might injure his dignity. Those who are manual workers or in domestic service find other means [of livelihood], for example as guardian of an orchard or of a mill, or in charge of children, going with them in the morning to their lessons and coming back [with them] in the evening, and anyone who wishes to pursue a course of studies or to devote himself to the religious life receives every aid to the execution of his purpose.

It is one of the laudable customs of the people of Damascus that not a man of them breaks his fast during the nights of Ramaḍān entirely alone. Those of the standing of amīrs, qāḍīs and notables invite their friends and [a number of] faqīrs to break fast at their houses. Merchants and substantial traders follow the same practice; the poor and the country folk for their part assemble each night in the house of one of their own number or in a mosque, each brings what he has, and they all break fast together.

* * *

The Mamlūks liked pomp and grandeur. Whether at court or traveling, in peace or in war, whether dispensing justice or banqueting, they put on a show which could hardly be surpassed. When in Damascus, the sultan would see to it that whatever he was accustomed to in Cairo was exhibited there also. When attending the Friday prayers at the Great Umayyad Mosque in Damascus, he himself ascertained that the *maqṣūrah* (a special chamber reserved for the ruler) was well decorated and well guarded; that in his procession to the mosque he was protected from the sun with his yellow silk parasol; that his gold-stitched saddle was used, or, if he walked, carried before him; that the flags with his name, titles, and inscriptions were properly carried; and that the exact number of drums and *ḳūsāt* (cymbals) accompanied the procession. When in the Hall of Justice, the sultan sat on a chair above all present, while his ministers, amirs, and judges sat on both sides.

The *nāyib al-ṣalṭana* in Damascus followed the example set by his master: his processions were ostentatious. Accompanied by his officers, who were dressed in red robes with large turbans on their heads, riding on horses with beautiful saddles, and covered with rich cloth hanging from both sides, the governor went to Maydān al-Khayl (square of the horses), Maydān Taḥt al-Qalʿa, al-Mizzah, or any of the suburban *maydāns*. There, he and his retinue trained their horses, practiced archery, or played polo *(sawalajan)*. On the return trip, the men accompanying the governor descended from their horses at different stages, beginning with the juniors among them, until the procession reached the official residence, where only the governor remained mounted. *Al-nāyib* then entered the great hall, where a special chair, covered with yellow satin and standing on a dais, was ready for him. Judges sat on the right and administrative officers on the left, while others took their places, seated or standing.

Complaints, written out on pieces of paper, were presented to the governor through a line of officials. He would then pronounce his judgments, which were recorded by a clerk and entrusted to the respective officials for execution. This was usually followed by a *simāṭ,* a sumptuous banquet, in which all present participated. In most cases, the affairs of state were discussed later with the close circle of advisers, amirs, and other officials, everyone else usually leaving after the meal.

As a city with the resources mentioned above, Damascus must have enjoyed its wealth, which undoubtedly could not have been evenly distributed. Public festivals were often occasions for royal banquets. To celebrate the Prophet's birthday, al-Muẓaffar (1308–1309) had 5,000 sheep and 10,000 fowls roasted, 100,000 bowls of vegetables cooked, and 30,000 dishes of sweetmeats served at a public banquet to which the general public was invited. Tinkiz, who was governor of Damascus for a number of years, left 730,000 dirhams and 2,700,000 dinars ($3,966,100), plus jewelry. A merchant, al-Kamāl by name, who died in 1236 left 300,000 dinars ($435,000) and 100 large pearls. Amat al-Laṭīf, a wealthy lady who passed away in 1245, left jewels worth about $50,000. In 1300, Damascus found no great difficulty in paying Ghāzān an indemnity of 4,000,000 dirhams ($280,000), except that intermediaries and agents demanded large amounts for themselves.

Needless to say, the people mentioned above represented a ruling class which had no scruples about how it collected its wealth. Merchants certainly controlled the markets and benefited from both ordinary profits and the fluctuation of prices. There were also times when they withheld their merchandise from the market, because of crop failure, a serious invasion, or excessive demands by foreign traders, to be sold at higher prices later or "under the counter" at the time. But what about the ordinary citizen who toiled to earn his living? An average Damascene family of Mamlūk era, composed of husband, wife, and four children, required the following essential commodities per month, exclusive of clothes and rent:

Commodity	*Amount (In Pounds)*	*Total Price (In Dollars)*
Wheat	150	$0.95
Rice	25	.21
Other cereals	25	.18
Meat	25	.85
Sugar	15	.90
Oil	20	.25
Vegetables	—	$0.30
		Total $3.64

Thus the head of such a family had to earn between $5.00 and $6.50 to provide for the basic needs of his wife, his children, and himself.

Unfortunately, I could not obtain data on the wages of skilled and semiskilled workmen and common laborers, but *waqfs,* at least in most cases, usually specified what was to be paid those who performed certain duties at a *madrasah,* a mosque, or a *bīmāristān*. Such information has been summed up in the following table.

Classification	*Monthly Salary (In Dollars)*
Physician	$21.00
Professor	5.60
Imam	2.80
Muezzin	2.10
Teacher of *ḥadīths*	2.10
Assistant teacher	1.40

Student	0.70
Qur'ān reader	1.00
Porter	$1.40

It is obvious that only a physician could live comfortably, and a professor would just barely make it. It should be added, however, that most subordinates received bread rations and were probably part-time workers on these jobs, but even then they could not, by any means, claim a standard of living which was to be envied.

In addition to the merchant class and the recipients of *waqf* money, there were also workmen and laborers (skilled and otherwise), farmers, government officials (except judges), and numerous other people who made up the population of the city. Information is lacking about most of these, but it may be surmised that with the existence of various charitable institutions, to which the poorer groups flocked, there were many chores and errands they could perform and thus eke out a living. It remains that only a small section of the inhabitants of the "noble city of Damascus," could enjoy life. Fortunately, the natural amenities of its surroundings provided its residents, then as well as now, with places for enjoyment that cost very little money.

As must have been the case in other periods, Damascus suffered hard times under the Mamlūks. Famines, droughts, and military campaigns led to hoarding and sharp rises in prices, situations which were not always brought under control. Below is a summary of such trends in the prices of essential foods in Damascus during the fourteenth and fifteenth centuries. The figures are proportional to normal prices provided by two political geographers of the period, al-'Umari and al-Qalqashandi.

Commodity	*Increase in Price (In Per Cent)*
Wheat	700–1,000
Barley	600–1,000
Rice	350– 400
Meat	500–1,800
Sugar	500
Fowls	600

·6·

City Administration

Most Muslim towns and cities had no elective bodies or magistrates, for Islam provided no special laws or codes for municipal organizations and practice did not develop one. One should remember, too, that medieval Muslim towns did not experience the struggle for freedom which their contemporaries in Europe underwent, and thus they did not evolve anything similar to the European municipal system. All Muslim city magistrates were chosen by the sovereign, and under the Mamlūks, such authority was vested in either the sultan himself or in his *nāyib*. Damascus was no exception; the magistrates who supervised its various activities and organized its municipal life were government appointees.

What officials did the city have? In other words, who governed the city, supervised its security, conducted its affairs, controlled its markets, and administered justice?

Damascus had a *wālī* (governor of a city), appointed by the sultan, but he was subordinate to the *nāyib al-ṣalṭana,* or provincial governor. The *wālī* was responsible for the security of the city and its people, and he attended to that personally as he inspected the *ḥārahs,* or quarters, of the city at night: he saw to it that evildoers were circumvented. His jurisdiction covered all Damascus, including the suburbs, but the citadel was excluded. The *wālī* had assistants who moved about the place, since there was no system of offices in various parts of the city. The *shurṭa* (police) and their chief were under his supervision, but on more than one occasion he himself would actually head the security organization. Quite often, a director of the *shurṭa* was authorized to wear a special headgear, and he could thus be easily recognized. All who were arrested were first brought before the head of the police for preliminary investigation. Although he was not, strictly speaking, a judge, he could dispense with cases where no violation of the Sharia was involved.

Like a number of great cities, then and now, Damascus harbored a number of people who could disturb the peace and cause the population a great deal of trouble. In order to keep such persons under control, the *wālī* had, besides the *shurṭa,* additional men to help him; he also had special methods of operation to which he could resort. *Aḥdāth* were stationed at places of importance during the night. The shaikh of the *ḥārah* was responsible for order locally.

Most Damascus streets were illuminated at night, and there was a group of people, known as *al-ḍaw'iya,* whose duty it was to keep the lamps burning. Residents were accustomed to the beating of drums at the citadel three times during the night, not only to indicate the hour, but also to warn the night watch to be wide awake.

When a murder was committed, the *wālī* often resorted to a system of collective punishment in which the people of the *ḥārah* in which it occurred were compelled to pay blood money, plus a fine, if they failed to produce the murderer. And the *wālī* saw to it that laws prohibiting trade in alcoholic beverages were enforced. He was also responsible for the safety of pilgrims for about fifty miles to the south of Damascus.

Qāḍis (judges) administered the law in the various districts of the city under the supervision of the chief justices of their rites. The Ayyūbids had restricted the post of chief justice to the Shāfi'ites and this practice was followed by the very early Mamlūks, but in 1266, Baybars ordained the appointment of four chief justices, not only in Cairo, but in Damascus and Aleppo as well. From then on, each of the four Sunnite rites (Shāfi'i, Ḥanafi, Ḥanbali, and Maliki) had its own chief justice, to whom the judges were attached, although often the post of the Malikite chief justice would be a sinecure. Damascus, because of its size and population, needed many judges to attend to the various legal cases.

A *qāḍi* administered Sharia, the body of which had been more or less discussed, classified, collated, and collected some five centuries before the Mamlūk era. He judged all cases, for there were no separate courts at that time, but one could say that most of these were concerned with questions of personal status. Commercial cases, pure and simple, were the concern of the administration and were dealt with expediently, not according to any prescribed law, especially when foreigners were involved. Christians and Jews went to their own ecclesiastical and rabbinical courts for matters of purely religious and personal character.

An interesting institution which existed in Damascus and

in numerous cities of the area was the *shuhūd* (literally, "witnesses"). Originally associated with the *qāḍi* to help decide a question of *'adāla* (equity), they had developed, between the eighth and tenth centuries, into a body of "notaries," who decided smaller disputes independently. In this capacity they were officers of the *qāḍi* and were appointed and dismissed by him. In the thirteenth century there was a widespread revival of the system. When al-Jamāl al-Miṣrī became judge of Damascus in 1220, he introduced the practice of collecting the *shuhūd* twice a week, on Tuesdays and Fridays, at the 'Adilīya Court, so that anyone who had a document to be attested or a dispute to be resolved could have it done on the spot. No specific qualifications, aside from being a devoted Muslim, were required of the *shuhūd*. Many of the Damascene *shuhūd* were booksellers and bookbinders, who, after finishing their usual work, proceeded to the houses of justice to attend to their judicial duties. Later it became customary to find *shuhūd* gathered in four places where they transacted business: Taḥt al-Sā'āt, al-Khizāna, Bāb al-Shāmīya, and Sūq Ṣārūja.

Within the circle of people concerned with justice was another official, known as *al-muftī,* whose duty was to assist in making a ruling when the case at hand did not fall within the coverage of known Sharia laws. Damascus, like Aleppo, had its own *muftī,* whose jurisdiction covered not only the city but the entire province. As it was, the *muftī* of Damascus was often invited to express opinions on questions sent from neighboring provinces, especially when the latter had no *muftī*. There is on record a very interesting case from the fourteenth century which illustrates this. In 1350 a group of European traders happened to be in Acre, and they were permitted to celebrate Easter Sunday in the town. They were assaulted and much trouble between them and some of the townspeople followed. They were arrested, but the governor of Acre did not know how to judge them. Were they to be dealt with like the native Christians, or were they people with a safe-conduct because they had come as traders? He requested a ruling from the *nāyib* of Ṣafad, to which Acre belonged administratively, but the latter could not solve the problem, and since the office of *muftī* was vacant at the time, the *nāyib* of Safad sought the opinion of the *muftī* of Damascus through its governor. Al-Subkī, the *muftī,* rendered a *fatwa* (legal opinion), stating that because it was in the interest of the empire to maintain good relations between the sultan and the cities of the traders, they should be considered as having a safe-conduct, which meant that they would receive a very mild punishment; it practically amounted to acquittal.

It is interesting to note that during times of invasion or siege, when the *wālī* had fled the city, so that none were legally responsible for its administration, a group of notables took it upon themselves to attend to its affairs. When Ghāzān's men entered Damascus in 1299, the magistrates had absconded, the men who stepped in were the *qāḍi,* the superintendent of the professors, a few *'ulamā* (theologians), and some of the shaikhs of the *ḥārahs*. There was no law or customary procedure regarding such matters, and this was not a solitary incident.

The smaller departments in city administration were headed by officials of junior status, known as *shāds*. The *wālī* was a Mamlūk and the head of the *shurṭa,* if not the *wālī* himself, was often a Mamlūk, but the *qāḍi,* the *shāds,* and the other officers were chosen from the native people. The *shāds* included *shād al-zakāh,* who collected alms from the financially obligated Muslims and in addition saw to it that spice merchants contributed their share of taxes to the treasury. *Shād al-awqāf* supervised the charitable endowments in the city, but only if no stipulation for their administration was made by the donor. The variety of the *waqfs* and the ways of spending them made this office an important one.

Four *shāds* supervised the glass, iron, and brass factories; Dār al-Biṭṭīkh wal-Fakiha (the Market of Melons and Fruits); the sugar refineries; and *al-ʿushūr* (customs). The factories were sultan-owned, and the *shāds* supervised the interests of the state, securing accurate inventories of merchandise. The fruit market contributed large sums to the *wālī* and his treasury, and the *shād* saw to it that these were collected regularly. Foreign traders carried goods to and from Damascus, and the *shād* secured the payment of customs by such merchants.

Two markets seem to have had a special place in the eyes of the provincial governor, not only because they yielded much to the treasury, but also because of their military and security aspects. They were Sūq al-Khayl (the Horse Market) and Sūq al-Raqīq (the Slave Market). The former was important because of the soldiers' need of horses, the vital means of transport in war, and slaves were strictly supervised, lest there be disguised spies among them, but also because it was in these markets that the richer and more influential Mamlūks sought future recruits—servants and bodyguards.

* * *

Social institutions in Damascus, such as *bīmāristāns,*

mosques, schools, and *zāwiyas,* had their own nazirs. It was not essential to have a physician as nazir of a *bīmāristān,* but it was important to have a man of character. He was responsible to the *nāyib al-ṣalṭana* for his actions and had in his charge the endowments of the hospital. The physicians, whether attached to a *bīmāristān* or practicing privately, were under the supervision of a chief or head physician. Damascus usually had three such people: chief of the physicians, chief of the surgeons, and chief of the oculists. Sometimes one of these, if especially eminent in his profession, would preside over the medical corps at large. Early in the thirteenth century Badr al-Dīn held such a position.

Sometime in the eleventh century, al-Yabrūdī, one of Damascus' most eminent physicians, formulated what might be considered the ethical code of the medical profession. This was strictly observed by those who practiced medicine in the city. It is of interest to include a summary of it here:

1. A physician should be sound of limb, intelligent, wise, and of good memory.
2. He should keep both his body and his clothes clean.
3. He must enjoy the confidence of his patients and should never betray such confidence.
4. The interest of the physician in curing his patients must have a greater weight than that of fees, and he should pay more attention to the poor than to the rich.
5. A physician must be ready to educate his fellow men, not just treat them.
6. He should not cast a covetous eye at things he sees in the houses of his clients.
7. He should be trustworthy; should not prescribe a poison-

ous medicine, neither should he teach its use. He must never exercise abortion. His attitude toward an enemy should not differ from that toward a friend or loved one.

Mosques were supervised by nazirs, khatibs, and imams. The first administered the *waqf* and saw to the maintenance of the building, the second delivered the Friday sermon and also taught, and the last-named led prayers. Because of its importance in Damascus and the surrounding area, the nazir of the Great Umayyad Mosque was often the chief justice of the city. To this high dignitary of the state was also assigned the care of all teaching posts in Damascus, both great and small. The former were obviously held by highly educated men, for it was just such men who kept the torch of learning alive in the great Syrian capital.

Although the *zāwiyas* were, among other things, centers of learning, they were not under the supervision of the chief justice: they were independent and had their own directors. Each *zāwiya,* irrespective of specific name, be it a *ḵhānqā* or *ribāṭ,* had its own shaikh, who supervised his own group or order. All shaikhs were under one head, known as shaikh of shaikhs, who acted both as controller of the fellows and as an intermediary with the authorities. These people were important to the state; they could create a religiously discontented public opinion if they chose to do so; but they did not. They elected to be allied with the sultan, and many sang his praises. The *zāwiyas,* however, were placed under strict surveillance, lest they should harbor Shī'ites or Ishmaelites; as it was, many of the inhabitants of the *zāwiyas* were vigilant in their search for these men. *Zāwiyas,* as centers of learning for the Sufis, contributed much to the literature and thought of the period, as we shall see later.

It has often been said that teachers of all ranks were in the service of the state, which was concerned with their choice, particularly those of the more influential positions, but we must bear in mind that a fairly large number of them would, at any time, prefer to resign their sometimes lucrative appointments and withdraw to their homes rather than submit to the whims of a ruler. This resulted from the fact that they viewed their profession with great respect and thought highly of their duties as keepers of the sciences of religion. This is quite clear from the names of those who accepted the posts of professors in the schools: they were the ranking *'ulamā* of the age.

* * *

The Mamlūk state recognized, as had apparently been recognized earlier, that it was easier to deal with the non-Muslim communities through special channels. After all, since they were given special status and were free to exercise their religious beliefs and practice their own rituals, they had to have their own organizations, at least where personal status and ecclesiastical matters were concerned.

The Christians had two *baṭraqs* (patriarchs) in Damascus, one for the Melchites and the other for the Jacobites. Both were responsible to the *nāyib* of the province, and their jurisdiction extended over all the followers of their respective rites, not only in Damascus or its province, but throughout the entire region. In the latter case, they were directly under the sultan.

The *baṭraq* was selected by his own community, but his

appointment had to be approved by the sultan. The charter of appointment said, among other things, that the *baṭraq* was "appointed, after their [the community's] choice, according to the rules of Christianity, as the controller of their affairs. . . . He should rule according to the laws of his denomination . . . treat them with mercy . . . try their cases according to their laws of inheritance and marriage. . . . He should observe his monks . . . archbishops, bishops and priests. . . . He is the final authority in matters of religion. . . . All parishes, churches, monasteries and convents are under his jurisdiction. . . . He should not harbour strangers of doubtful character, and should never conceal from the sultan any letters received by him from any of the [foreign] kings. He should beware of ever going to meet them [the foreign kings]." The community was enjoined to "obey his [the *baṭraq's*] orders and abide by his instructions. He should not permit the Christians to ring bells in their churches, nor to chant aloud when performing their rituals, especially when Muslims are being called to prayer. He must see that Christians wear the prescribed clothes."

The head of the Jewish community was known as the *nāgid* earlier, but later the word *ra'īs* (or *rayyis*), meaning "head" or "chief,' became more common. The Samaritans, of whom there was a sizable group in Damascus, also had their own religious chief, but the *ra'īs* of the community was in Nablus. In his charter of appointment, the *ra'īs* of the Jews was given approximately the same duties as his counterpart.

Both the *baṭraq* and the Jewish *ra'īs* had assistants of various degrees. Bishops and clergy acted on behalf of the former, while the latter was aided by a parnas, who supervised alms collections, elders, *hāber* or *dayān* (observers), hazzans, and *bet-dīn* (judges), each of whom performed his duties as prescribed by Jewish law.

Neither the *baṭraq* nor the *ra'īs* was responsible for the collection of the *jizyah* (poll tax), which was paid directly to the government official in charge of such collections. In order to ascertain such dues, however, the state had to be acquainted with development within the non-Muslim communities. A government official known as *shād al-jawāli* (supervisor of religious communities) saw to it that the heads of Christians, Jews, and Samaritans supplied him with *riqā* (reports) containing detailed information—including names, of course—on people normally residing in their districts, newcomers, births, deaths, departures, and converts to Islam.

This system of granting some sort of autonomy to the various religious communities solved a number of administrative problems and enabled such communities to develop their own societies. In a way, however, it encouraged religious and ethnic segregations—and also made it easier for the governors to locate them in time of need, whatever the cause might be.

* * *

The markets and trades were absolutely the most important concern of the Mamlūk government. Damascus was a large city, so there was the problem of providing the inhabitants with necessary provisions. Essentially, the purveyors of these items were people living near by, although more durable goods were supplied by merchants from more distant lands, including international traders. Prices were subject not only to supply and demand but also to a number of factors connected with the methods of sale, the differences in weights and measures, and the varied currencies then in use. For Damascus, in its capacity as a city dealing in goods from areas far and wide, used not less than three different measures for cereals, two others for oils and liquids, and four different kinds of weights. To this must be added the fact that Damascus used three kinds of currency. The Mamlūks, following the practice of Muslim states throughout history, had a dual currency: the gold dinar (worth $1.45), which was always rather scarce, and the silver dirham (worth $0.07), which was more often in use. The relation of the latter to the former differed according to the amount of silver used in the dirham, the best coins being those known as *nuqra,* which were two-thirds silver and one-third copper, in which case, usually, 20 dirhams were equal to one dinar. A copper coin known as *fils,* of which 48 were equal to a dirham, was struck by the Mamlūks, but it was never accepted as a standard currency, basically because it was soon debased. May it be added that another type of dinar, used in calculating the remuneration of military personnel, existed in theory. And three foreign currencies were frequently used in Damascus: *al-ifranti* (apparently a French coin equal to 17 dirhams, or $1.19), the Venetian gold (worth $1.40) and silver (worth $0.14) ducats, and the bezant, equal to 10 dirhams ($0.70).

Who was in charge of these and similar areas of activity? May the reader be reminded that certain markets, the horse market and the slave market, for example, and some industries, such as those of sugar and iron, had superintendents who were state agents. But the real burden of looking after the markets, the tradesmen, and the merchants fell upon the shoulders of *al-muḥtasib.*

The Greeks introduced into the cities of the Near East an office whose holder was known as the agoranome, or inspector of markets. His duties included ascertaining that the merchandise sold in the markets was of good quality and that proper weights and measures were used. This office continued under the Romans and Byzantines and was apparently inherited by the Muslims, along with many other administrative offices, after their conquest of the area. Syrian towns seem to have continued the practice, but from the tenth or eleventh century on, the position was a religious office, as were a number of other posts.

Also after the eleventh century, another development concerning *al-muḥtasib* occurred, namely, the appearance of numerous handbooks which explained the legal and religious nature of the office, set the necessary qualifications for its holder, and specified his duties. Under the Ayyūbids and the Mamlūks, *al-muḥtasib* was considered one of the most influential officeholders, for he watched subversive movements or individuals. The Damascus *muḥtasib* was no exception; if anything, he held a greater responsibility.

The appointee for the office was chosen carefully: he had to be a *faqīh,* with great knowledge of the law, pious, clean in heart, strict, patient, and well acquainted with the methods of artisans and their ways of deception. He was expected to respect the privacy of people. His duties were numerous. He had a special *dikka* (booth) and remained close to the *sūqs,* riding through them and surprising merchants day and night;

his assistants and servant boys accompanied him on his tours. He appointed *'arīfs* (supervisors) to look after the markets (they were actually chiefs of the trades, for each trade usually had its own market). Although the *muḥtasib* performed most of his work at the markets, he also frequented mosques to see that responsible people kept them clean and that those using them behaved themselves. Lonely lanes were to be kept under close observation, lest men and women use them as trysting places.

Al-muḥtasib saw to it that markets and streets were kept clean and that passers-by were not hampered by goods stacked in their way. He protected the general public against bad food, false measures and weights, fraudulent money-changers, the monopolizing or hoarding of goods, and children against harsh penal punishment by their teachers. It was also his duty to safeguard the public from fraudulent practices by physicians, oculists, surgeons, and pharmacists. Directly or otherwise, he supervised butchers, fish friers, makers of sweetmeats and sausage, weavers, potters, needle makers, henna sellers, workers in sesame-oil presses, sieve makers, tanners, felt makers, makers of reed mats, sellers of trinkets, rice merchants, and water carriers.

Thus *al-muḥtasib* was an important officer of the state whose duties were based on two things: he was entrusted with the protection of the public against all fraudulent dealings and injustices, and he was to ascertain that people carrying provisions and goods to the city were not met outside the walls by local buyers who would purchase the goods at cheap prices to make large profits through exorbitant prices. All sales were to be made in the market through a *dallāl* (auctioneer) under the supervision of one of *al-muḥtasib*'s men. Although he could not set prices, *al-muḥtasib* saw to it that exorbitant prices were not charged. It was one of his foremost responsibilities to see that wheat, flour, and bread were available for consumers. But one should bear in mind that *al-muḥtasib* also protected the government. Artisans, mainly of what may be called middle-class people or so, were under his control, that is, the control of the government. This is understandable when one remembers that people of this class were prone to be influenced by Shī'ite and Ishmaelite teachings, a matter of great concern to a Sunnite state.

There were a few walks of life where the shadow of *al-muḥtasib* did not fall. I have referred to the *sūqs* and factories, and now I may add that higher education was not his concern. Insofar as these matters were under control—the former group being supervised by nazirs and the latter being the responsibility of the chief justices—the government had no anxiety about them. It was the freer and lesser trades and professions which were to be watched carefully.

Al-muḥtasib could inflict punishments, especially when the *shurṭa* were assigned to his office, but this was resorted to only after frequent admonitions. It seems that in this capacity, *al-muḥtasib* acted as a judge of criminal cases which did not need to go to court, and certainly he acted according to the injunctions of the Sharia.

·7·

Intellectual Life

By THE BEGINNING of the eleventh century the Fatimids had already annexed a large part of Syria and Shī'ism had spread to many parts of the country. When late in the same century and early in the following one the Crusaders founded Latin states in Syria, Lebanon, and Palestine, Islam suffered political defeat. But the twelfth century brought a Muslim reaction; begun by Zangi, it was strengthened by Nūr al-Dīn, and under the leadership of Saladin, Muslim forces defeated the Latins at Ḥiṭṭīn in 1187.

Zangi, Nūr al-Dīn, and Saladin were Sunnites, and the revival of Islam at their hands meant a revival of Sunnism. Nūr al-Dīn, according to Abū Shāma, supported Sunnism in Aleppo, changed the innovation of *adhān* (the call to prayer) and suppressed the *rafidis* (apostates). Saladin put an end to the Fatimid caliphate in 1171, when the caliph of Baghdad was again recognized in Egypt and Syria. In their enthusiasm for promoting Sunnism, the Zangids and Ayyūbids saw to it that all possible measures were taken for the suppression of Shī'ism; schools were founded to teach Sunnism, and the office of *muḥtasib* was revived. The Mamlūks followed the policy of their predecessors; they completed the political and military campaigns against the Crusaders and reconquered Syria. In addition, they founded more schools, organized the government, tightened its hold on the people, and placed almost all walks of life under strict control. They waged wars against the Nuṣayris and arranged for Sunnite mosques to be built in their lands.

Saladin and his successors were Shāfi'ites, and this rite, which had allied itself with Ash'arism, became a sort of state rite. Baybars became the first sultan to recognize officially the four Sunnite rites when he appointed four chief justices, first in Cairo and later in Syria. Thus Sunnism emerged victorious, having secured the full alliance of the state, which, in turn, needed the Sunnite *'ulamā* to support it.

The other movement which was influential in the period under discussion is Sufism. Essentially an attempt by individuals to establish, through a life of piety and asceticism, contact with the Creator, Sufism gradually developed into a movement of far-reaching influence on religious thought in Islam. "The ascetics," says one writer, "were the forerunners and they were known throughout Arabia, Iraq, Palestine, Syria and Khorasan, and the virtues they stood for and according to which they lived included *zuhd* (self-denial) and total disregard of wealth and ambitious living. Ascetics were negative in their attitude to life and their existence could be joyless. But warmth soon crept into the life of many ascetics—warmth caused by a searching light and spiritual elation. Here Baghdad was the prime contributor and remained so for some time." And it is rather interesting to note that in this, Baghdad followed its own earlier leadership in literature, theology, law, and philosophy.

The number of Sufis increased, and finally they fell under theosophical influences from the Greeks, Indians, Christians, and other systems of thought, so that eventually, what had been individual views of Sufis gradually developed into theories and systems with their own adherents and expounders, which I have no intention of discussing here.

A further development in the history of Sufism was the growth of orders, or *ṭarīqahs,* the most original of which were al-Qādirīya (founded in Baghdad by 'Abd al-Qādir al-Jilānī, who died in 1166); al-Suhrawardīya (founded by al-Suhrawardī, who died in 1234); al-Shāḍhilīya (founded in North Africa by al-Shāḍhilī, who died in 1258), the first North African order; and al-Mawlawīya (founded by Jalāl al-Dīn al-Rumi, who died in Turkey in 1273), whose members are commonly known as the dancing dervishes. From these four, as well as others, scores of orders derived.

Insofar as Sufism contained teachings which were not acceptable to the orthodox *'ulamā,* it is no wonder that Sufis incurred the wrath of the latter, who accused them of *shirk* (polytheism) and finally *kufr* (infidelity). One scholar points out that "the basic difference, in attitude, between the 'ulamā and the Ṣūfīs is that the former considered 'ilm (science, i.e., of legal interpretation) of the Qur'ān and the Ḥadīth as the only way of knowing God and getting inspiration to follow His path and commandments, while the latter thought of ma'rifa (knowledge, or gnosis) as a way for achieving the same end. The Ṣūfī ma'rifa, although not discarding the pillars of Islam, emphasized the personal experience and gradually marked various ḥāls (states) and maqāms (stations) along which Ṣūfī proceeded towards the gnosis of God. A Ṣūfī developed ḥāls, spiritual moods, as he progressed along the pilgrim's spiritual path from one maqām to another. And this path was long, circuitous, arduous and demanding with its 45 stages from tawba (conversion) to shawq (yearning) to be constantly with God." Needless to say, it was not given to many people to attain the highest of these goals, but even partial success brought the person nearer to God than the legalist interpretation, or so the Sufis held.

Sufism, however, possessed one outstanding Muslim jurist who succeeded in reconciling, at least in his own mind, the Sufi and Sunnite philosophies. Al-Ghazālī (d.1111) was one of the greatest, if not the greatest, of the *'ulamā* of his day when he decided to practice Sufism experimentally. The result was astounding: not only did al-Ghazālī accept Sufism, he declared himself its champion! This was Sufism's greatest conquest. Al-Ghazālī himself has told the story of his conversion in his spiritual autobiography, entitled *al-Munqidh min al-ḍalāl*. In part of this work he says:

> Then I turned my attention to the Way of the Ṣūfīs. I knew that it could not be traversed to the end without both doctrine and practice, and that the gist of the doctrine lies in overcoming the appetites of the flesh and getting rid of its evil dispositions and vile qualities, so that the heart may be cleared of all but God; and the means of clearing it is *dhikr Allah,* that is, commemoration of God and concentration of every thought upon Him. Now, the doctrine was easier to me than the practice, so I began by learning their doctrine from the books and sayings of their Shaykhs, until I acquired as much of

> their Way as it is possible to acquire by learning and hearing, and saw plainly that what is most peculiar to them cannot be learned, but can only be reached by immediate experience and ecstasy and inward transformation. I became convinced that I had now acquired all the knowledge of Sufism that could possibly be obtained by means of study; as for the rest, there was no easy way of coming to it except by leading the mystical life. I looked on myself as I then was. Worldly interests encompassed me on every side. Even my work as a teacher—the best thing I was engaged in—seemed unimportant and useless in view of the life hereafter. When I considered the intention of my teaching, I perceived that instead of doing it for God's sake alone I had no motive but the desire for glory and reputation. I realised that I stood on the edge of a precipice and would fall into Hellfire unless I set about to mend my ways. . . . Conscious of my helplessness and having surrendered by will entirely, I took refuge with God as a man in sore trouble who has no resource left. God answered my prayer and made it easy for me to turn my back on reputation, and wealth and wife and children and friends.

Through his conversion to Sufism, al-Ghazālī assured the "mystical or introspective attitude a place within official Islam side by side with the legalism of the lawyers and the intellectualism of the theologians." But he also Sunnized Sufism, for Sufism he accepted was not that of extremist Sufis. As Professor A. J. Arberry has said, from al-Ghazālī's time on, at least a "sober" type of Sufism was accepted as a Muslim science. This observation happens to have numerous exceptions, however, and one of these was Ibn Taymīyah, the Damascene *'ālim* of our period, who launched attacks on Sufism. But more of this later.

In the thirteenth century, Islamic mysticism had created its own theosophy, by acquiring the idea of the logos, which was henceforth applied to *al-Ḥaqīqat al-Muḥammadīya* (the Idea of Muḥammad). Two Sufis expounded this: Ibn al-Fāriḍ (d.1235 in Cairo) and Ibn 'Arabi (d.1240 in Damascus).

Damascus was, in the thirteenth through the fifteenth centuries, a center of Islamic thought in both of its aspects, the legalistic Sunnite tradition and the Sufi tradition, with the scales tilted in favor of the former.

A number of factors led to this. I have referred to the "new order of things" several times, and I must now add that the imminent danger of the Mongol invasion—and later the Mongol conquest of Baghdad—drove many learned men westward from the 'Abbāsid capital. Damascus was a natural destination for them. The patronage of the Zangids, the Ayyūbids, and some Mamlūk sultans attracted men from northern Iraq to Damascus. The family of Ibn Taymīyah, migrated to Damascus when the future *'ālim* was a baby, but his father and his grandfather had been among the renowned *'ulamā*. Somehow, Cairo could not always accommodate men of letters at that time; Ibn 'Arabi left the country after a few attempts on his life; Ibn Khaldūn remained there only on sufferance, as one sees from his autobiography. Damascus was attractive. Also being a wealthy city, it provided people wtih means of livelihood. Last but not least, there was the migration of a number of *'ulamā* from Palestine in the twelfth century, such as Banu Qudāma, who founded al-Ṣāliḥīyah. Aleppo certainly continued to be a center of learning, but Damascus ran far ahead.

I have been able to obtain the names of 135 learned men

who spent their lives, or parts thereof, in Syria, but by far the majority of them lived in Damascus. They may be classified as follows:

Fuqaha' (jurisconsults)	26
Expositors of the Qur'ān, dogmatists, and traditionalists	23
Sufis	5
Linguists, men of letters, and poets	32
Historians and geographers	28
Physicians, scientists, and astronomers	14
Encyclopedists	4
Miscellaneous writers	3

The first three classes, that is, men who wrote on subjects of purely religious nature, 54 in number, comprised 40 per cent of the total number of *'ulamā*.

With regard to books, I have sought out the 918 titles written during the period. They may be classified by subject, as follows:

Fiqh	271
Exposition of the Qur'ān, dogma, and traditions	164
Sufism	158
Language and literature, including poetry	135
History and geography	123
Medicine, sciences, and astronomy	52
Encyclopedias	4
Miscellaneous works	11

Works on religious subjects number 593 and comprise about 65 per cent of the total number.

I would like to add a few remarks:

1. Many of the poetical works may be considered as dealing

with religious subjects when their theme was praise of the Prophet.

2. Many of the religious works run into several volumes, while books on sciences were usually shorter works. *Al-Jawāb al-Ṣāḥīḥ,* Ibn Taymīyah's *Fatāwa,* and Ibn Kathīr's *Tafsīr* (*Exposition*) are books of many volumes, to mention only a few examples.

3. There was a large number of *muḥaddithīn* (traditionalists), *qārīs* (readers of the Qur'ān), and imams who taught in schools and mosques but did not write any books; they should be taken into consideration.

If we bear in mind books which have been completely lost, name and all, we are justified in describing the literary production of the period as energetic and voluminous. And examination of some of the works relating to the defense of Islam or dealing with non-Sunnites or non-Muslims reveals that their authors were vigorous writers.

The period under discussion produced little scientific literature, with the exception of a few works on medicine and astronomy. There are two books on logic, twelve on geography, one on science, and one on military strategy and tactics. Medicine throve during the period because of the patronage of Nūr al-Dīn, Saladin, and their successors. Moreover, medicine was of practical use and did not interfere with matters of state. Similarly, most works on astronomy or allied branches deal with the practical side of the matter, such as the making of astrolabes.

Can one find an explanation for all this?

The state controlled higher education. Its aim was to defend its own existence, and this was the assigned task of religious teachers and thinkers, known collectively as *'ulamā,* or generally, "theologians." Freedom of thought had no place in the educational system of the period, neither was it allowed in intellectual life in general. Saladin, according to Abū Shāma, hated philosophers and those who opposed orthodoxy, so much so that he ordered the execution of al-Suhrawardī (al-Maqtūl). This was a dangerous precedent to be set by the idol of many of his successors.

Education became a matter of thoroughly understanding a theological system which the *'ulamā* took some pains to build. Both circles of learners and subjects of learning became narrow and restricted; one notes that many of the books on dogma were commentaries, explanations, and *dhuyūl* (continuations) to some one work. Linguistic books were of similar nature. Since the Islamic community received no new currents of thought during the thirteenth century and after, there were no stimulants to intellectual speculation. An internal equilibrium had been attained, and the theology of the age met the needs of the community it served. A change must come as a reaction against an impact from outside, and this was lacking throughout the Mamlūk reign.

During the conflict between Muslims and Crusaders, Arabic poetry flourished. The battles and victories of Nūr al-Dīn and Saladin gave poets topics for their work, and they never failed to sing the praises of the great princes. Ibn 'Unayn and Ibn al-Sā'ātī praised the Ayyūbids, although the first suffered banishment from Damascus and lived in exile in Yemen —but at the court of an Ayyūbid.

Poets of our period proper—the thirteenth and fourteenth centuries—who may be considered Syrians are numerous:

there are twenty-three of them. Their literary output, however, as far as quality is concerned, does not rank with productions of earlier periods of Arabic poetry. Ibn Nubāta is probably the best known. Born in Mayāfārqīn in 1287, he came to Damascus in 1316 but finally settled in Cairo, where he died in 1366. His *dīwān* contains a number of "praise" poems, eighteen of which begin with the traditional love or remembrance verses. Ibn Nubāta wrote *muwashshaḥ,* the new strophic measures, said to have been introduced to the East by Ibn 'Arabi. Another matter to be borne in mind is that he wrote poetry in *zajal,* an example of which is to be found in his *dīwān.*

Apparently, men of letters of the period felt the tendency of thinkers to spend their life in studying matters of theology, so that Yāqūt found it necessary to insert in the preface of his work, *Irshād al-Arīb* (*Dictionary of Learned Men*), an apology for writing on a nontheological subject:

> I am well aware of odious critics who will revile and disparage men, men whose mind has been poisoned by ignorance and whose inmost soul revolts against generous gifts of nature, declaring that it is of more importance to devote oneself to matters of religion and more useful in this world and the next. Do they know that men are fashioned in different moulds and with different capacities? God has appointed for every science men to preserve it in its completeness and bring order into its substance, and every man is guided to that for which he is created. I do not deny that were I to cleave to my mosque and my prayer-mat such conduct would be better adapted to the path of safety in the future life. But to pursue the best has been denied to me, and surely it suf-

fices to a man for virtue that he does nothing reprehensible and walks not in the way of deceit.

Ibn 'Arabi, the great Sufi of the late twelfth and early thirteenth centuries, spent the last twenty or so years of his life in Damascus, where he produced some of the most valuable of his works. He was born in Murcia (Andalusia) in 1165, received his early education in traditions and jurisprudence in Lisbon, Seville, and Ceuta, and traveled extensively in North Africa. It was in Tunis that he was initiated into Sufism, although he must have become acquainted with it earlier. Apparently, this new development eventually forced him to move eastward, for the age of the Almohades was not too encouraging for ideas which Ibn 'Arabi was already expressing. Besides, as a pious Muslim, he certainly wanted to perform the pilgrimage. So, at the age of thirty-eight, Ibn 'Arabi began his journey to the East.

His stay in Egypt was not very comfortable and his life was threatened several times, but Mecca appealed to him mightily and he enjoyed both the inhabitants and the pilgrims. During the eight years he spent there, he was busy writing and teaching, but more seriously he busied himself developing his speculative system, if one may say so. Later he visited Baghdad, which he liked but in which he did not stay—he probably saw the writing on the wall. After some short visits to Asia Minor, he finally settled in Damascus, where he died in 1240.

Fortunately for Ibn 'Arabi and for us, he was well received, well provided for, and well protected in Damascus. No less a person than Chief Justice Ibn al-Zakī was his patron, who, in admiration of the great Sufi, served him personally. The freer atmosphere of Damascus, compared to that of Cairo and the Muslim West, was both appealing to him and conducive to serious literary production, for it was here that he completed his *Futūḥāt* and *Fuṣūs*.

Ibn 'Arabi left many works; more than two hundred of the four hundred to seven hundred attributed to him have survived. True, most of them were short tracts, but there are bulky treatises, such as *al-Futūḥāt al-Makkīya,* a real Sufi encyclopedia, and *Fuṣūs al-Ḥikam,* which are the basis of his fame. Ibn 'Arabi was not, however, merely a writer; he was also a poet, and his *Nafḥ al-Ṭīb* testifies to this.

What was the philosophical system of this great Sufi? Ibn 'Arabi "gathered into the comprehensive range of his meditation the entire learning of Islam, and was perfectly familiar not only with the writings and teachings of the orthodox Sunni theologians, lawyers and philosophers, and of the Ṣūfīs from the earliest times to his own day, but also with the schismatic and heretical movements like the Muz'tazilites, Carmathians and Ismā'īlis. His system, vast and widely ranging as it is, embraces the speculations and terminologies of all his widely various sources; so that the problem of abstruse reference is complicated by the further constant difficulty of an inconsistent technical vocabulary."

It is obviously impossible in a few paragraphs even to hint at more than a minute fraction of Ibn 'Arabi's multifarious teachings, but the following notes will indicate how he relates to some of his predecessors and influences his successors.

1. God is Absolute Being and is the sole source of all Existence; in Him alone Being and Existence are one and inseparable.

2. The Universe possesses Relative Being, either actual or potential; it is both eternal-existent and temporal-nonexistent as being external to God.

3. God is both transcendent and immanent, transcendence and immanence being two fundamental aspects of Reality as man knows it. The *Ḥaqq* (Reality), of whom transcendence is asserted, is the same as the *Khalq* (Creation), of whom immanence is asserted, although (logically) the creator is distinguished from the created.

4. Being, apart from God, exists by virtue of God's Will, acting in accordance with the laws proper of the things thus existent; His agents are the Divine Names of universal concepts.

5. Before coming into existence, things of the phenomenal world were latent in the Mind of God as fixed prototypes (*a'yān thābita*) and were thus one with the Divine Essence and Consciousness; these prototypes are intermediaries between the One as Absolute Reality and the Phenomenal World.

6. There is no such thing as Union with God in the sense of becoming one with God, but there is the realization of the already existing fact that the mystic *is* one with God.

7. The creative, animating and rational principle of the Universe, or the First Intellect, is the Reality (Idea) of Muḥammad (*al-Ḥaqīqat al-Muḥammadīya*), also called the Reality of Realities (*Ḥaqīqat al-Ḥaqā'iq*); this principle finds its fullest manifestation in the Perfect Man (*al-Insān al-Kāmil*).

8. Each prophet is *a* Logos of God; *the* Logos is Muḥammad, the "head" of the hierarchy of prophets. All these individual logoi are united in the Reality of Muḥammad.

9. The Perfect Man is a miniature of Reality; he is the

microcosm, in whom are reflected all the perfect attributes of the macrocosm. Just as the Reality of Muhammad was the *creative principle* of the Universe, so the Perfect Man was the *cause* of the Universe, being the epiphany of God's desire to be known; for only the Perfect Man knows God, loves God, and is loved by God. For Man alone the world was made.

Ibn 'Arabi's style bespeaks of a great deal of complexity, ambiguity, and confusion, and his readers are irritated and baffled. Was all this the natural result of the great range of his thinking, spiritual experience, and meditation, or did he deliberately resort to this style in order to conceal from his contemporaries things which they could not accept, feeling that his ideas should be set down in writing? With this warning about his style in Arabic, the original language in which he wrote, I venture to place before the reader a few passages in translation. In *Fuṣūs al-ḥikam,* Ibn 'Arabi said: "God is never seen immaterially, and the vision of Him in woman is the most perfect of all." The following lines, from *Tarjumān al-Ashwāq,* are understandable in the light of this saying (the translation is by E. G. Browne):

> My soul is much concerned with Her,
> Although Her face I cannot see;
> Could I behold Her face indeed,
> Slain by Her blackened brows I'd be;
> And when my sight upon Her fell,
> I fell a captive to my Sight,
> And passed the night bewitched by Her,
> And still did rave when dawn grew bright.
> Alas! for my resolves so high!
> Did high resolve avail, I say,

The beauty of that Charmer shy,
Would not have made me thus to stray.
In beauty as a tender fawn,
Whose pasture the Wild Asses ken;
Whose coy regard and half-turned head
Make captives of the souls of Men!
Her breath so sweet as it would seem
As fragrant musk does yield delight.
She's radiant as the midday Sun:
She's as the Moon's Effulgence bright.
If She appear, She doth reveal
The splendor of the Morning fair;
If She Her tresses loose, the Moon
Is hidden by Her night-black hair.
Take Thou my heart, but leave, I pray,
O Moon, athwart the darkest Night,
Mine Eyes, that I may gaze on Thee.
For all my joy is in my sight!

The great Sufi often commented on his own writings. The following, also from *Tarjumān,* is a quotation with a summary of the comment:

> On the day of parting they did not saddle the full-grown reddish-white camels until they had mounted the peacocks upon them.
>
> Peacocks with murderous glances and sovereign power: thou wouldst fancy that each of them was a Bilqis on her throne of pearls.
>
> When she walks on the glass pavement thou seest a sun, a celestial sphere in the bosom of Idris.
>
> When she kills with her glances, her speech restores to life, as tho' she, in giving life thereby, were Jesus.

Commentary

The full-grown camels, that is the actions inward and outward, for they exalt the good word to Him who is throned on high, as He hath said: "And the good deed exalts it" [Koran XXXV, 2]. "The peacocks" mounted on them are his loved ones: he likens them to peacocks because of their beauty. The peacocks are the spirits of those actions, for no action is acceptable or good or fair until it hath a spirit consisting in the intention or desire of its doer.

"With murderous glances and sovereign power": he refers to the Divine wisdom which accrues to a man in his hours of solitude, and which assaults him with such violence that he is unable to behold his personality.

"A Bilqis on her throne of pearls": he refers to that which was manifested to Gabriel and to the Prophet during his night journey upon the bed of pearl and jacinth in the terrestrial heaven. The author calls the Divine wisdom "Bilqis" on account of its being the child of theory, which is subtle, and practice, which is gross, just as Bilqis was both spirit and woman, since her father was of the Jinn and her mother was of mankind.

The mention of Idris alludes to her lofty and exalted rank. "In the bosom of Idris," that is, under his control, in respect of his turning her wheresoever he will, as the Prophet said: "Do not bestow wisdom on those who are unworthy of it, lest ye do it a wrong." The opposite case is that of one who speaks because he is dominated by his feeling (*hāl*), and who is therefore under the control of an influence (*wārid*). In this verse the author calls attention to his puissance in virtue of a prophetic heritage, for the prophets are masters of their spiritual feelings (*ahwāl*), whereas most of the saints are mastered by them.

"She kills with her glances": referring to the station of passing-away in contemplation (*al-fanā fi 'l-mushāhada*). "Her speech restores to life": referring to the completion of the moulding of man when the spirit was breathed into him.

The following few verses represent both the feelings and the intellectual attitude of Ibn 'Arabi toward love in the very abstract, all-encompassing sense:

Within my heart, all forms may find a place,
The cloisters of the monk, the idol's fane
A pasture for gazelles, the Sacred House
Of God, to which all Muslims turn their face:
The tables of the Jewish Law, the Word
Of God, revealed unto His Prophet true.
Love is the faith I hold, and whereso'e'r
His camels turn, the one true faith is there.

From Ibn 'Arabi's *al-Futūḥāt al-Makkīya* comes the following example of his own revelations:

The veils of darkness and light, by which God is veiled from the world, are only what describes the contingent, because it is in the midst and it looks only to itself and it does not look to what is within the veil. If the veils were raised from the contingent the contingency would be revealed and the necessary and the imaginable, because the veil is raised, but the veils continue to be a concealment, and it must be so. Consider this world in regard to the raising of the veil, for He spoke of consuming, by the glory of His countenance, the creature who apprehends it and sometimes He says of Himself that the creatures can see Him and not be consumed, declaring that the veils are raised in the Vision, and the Vision itself is a veil. "The eye of His creature does not see Him," and if men understood the meaning of this, they would know themselves, and if they knew themselves, they would know God: and if they really knew God, they would be satisfied with Him and would think about Him alone, not about the kingdom of the heavens and the earth. If, indeed, they knew the truth of the matter, they would realize that He is Himself the Essence of the kingdom of the heavens and the earth.

If it were not for the Light, nothing at all could be apprehended by the mind or the senses or the imagination, and the name given to the Light, varies with the faculties, which we also call by different names. According to the common folk, the name is given to the mind, and among the gnostics, to the light of perception; when you apprehend what is audible, you call the light which apprehends, hearing, and when you apprehend what is visible, you call the light seeing. Light involves a relationship, for apprehending what is apparent. Everyone who perceives must have some relationship to the light, by which he is made able to perceive, and everything which is perceived has a relationship with God, Who is Light, that is, all which perceives and all which is perceived.

Ibn 'Arabi wrote a book called *Kitāb al-Ajwiba,* the *Book of Answers,* in which he tried to explain his views as if he were answering questions put to him. Here is a passage from this book:

He is and there is with Him no before or after, nor above nor below, nor far nor near, nor union nor division, nor how nor where nor place. He is now as He was, He is the One without oneness and the Single without singleness. He is the very existence of the First and the very existence of the Last, and the very existence of the Outward and the very existence of the Inward. So that there is no first nor last nor outward nor inward except Him, without their becoming Him or His becoming them. He is not in a thing nor a thing in Him, whether entering in or proceeding forth. It is necessary that you know Him, after this fashion, not by learning (*'ilm*) nor by intellect, nor by understanding, nor by imagination, nor by sense, nor by the outward eye nor by the inward eye, nor by perception. By Himself He sees Himself and by Himself He knows Himself. His veil, that is, phenomenal existence, is but the concealment of His existence in His oneness, without any attribute. There is no other and there is no existence for any other, than He. He whom you think to be other than God, he is not other than God, but you do not know Him and do not understand that you are seeing Him. He is still Ruler as well as ruled, and Creator as well as created. He is now as He was, as to His creative power and as to His sovereignty, not requiring a creature nor a subject. When He called into being the things that are, He was already endowed with all His attributes and He is as He was then. In His oneness there is no difference between what is recent and what is original: the recent is the result of His manifestation of Himself and the original is the result of His remaining within Himself.

There is no existence save His existence. To this the Prophet pointed when he said: "Revile not the world, for God is the world," pointing to the fact that the existence of the world is God's existence without partner or like or equal. It is related that the Prophet declared that God said to Moses: "O My servant, I was sick and thou didst not visit Me: I asked help of thee and thou didst not give it to Me," and other like expressions. This means that the existence of the beggar is His existence and the existence of the sick is His existence.

Now when this is admitted, it is acknowledged that this existence is His existence and that the existence of the sick is His existence. Now when this is admitted, it is acknowledged that this existence is His existence and that the existence of all created things, both accidents and substances, is His existence, and when the secret of one atom of the atoms is clear, the secret of all created things, both outward and inward, is clear, and you do not see in this world or the next, anything except God, for the existence of these two Abodes and their name, and what they name, all of them are assuredly He.

When the mystery—of realizing that the mystic is one with the Divine—is revealed to you, you will understand that you are no other than God and that you have continued and will continue without when and without times. Then you will see all your actions to be His actions and all your attributes to be His attributes and your essence to be His essence, though you do not thereby become He or He you, in either the greatest or the least degree. "Everything is perishing save His Face," that is, there is nothing except His Face, "then, whithersoever you turn, there is the Face of God."

Just as he who dies the death of the body, loses all his attributes, both those worthy of praise and those worthy of condemnation alike, so in the spiritual death all attributes, both those worthy of praise and those to be condemned, come to an end, and in all the man's states what is Divine comes to take the place of what was mortal. Thus, instead of his own essence, there is the essence of God in place of his own qualities, there are the attributes of God. He who knows himself sees his whole existence to be the Divine existence, but does not realize that any change has taken place in his own nature or qualities. For when you know yourself, your "I-ness" vanishes and you know that you and God are one and the same.

Ibn 'Arabi's influence on later Muslim thought can be traced in a number of trends. Sufis, even those who did not accept, or pretended not to have accepted, his pantheistic teachings, fell under his spell, drawing copiously on his doctrine of love. Even Cairo, which had earlier made his stay there uncomfortable, found a great deal in him, and about the turn of the century, many of its ardent Sufis were staunch supporters of his views. Equally interesting is the activity he stimulated among the *'ulamā,* who criticized him, for such a task was not easy. Later Muslim writers and authors differed greatly in evaluating him, and the major reason lies in the variety and depth of his spiritual and intellectual experiences and meditations.

Ibn 'Arabi also influenced medieval Christian mysticism, and his teachings could easily be accommodated within the framework of Christian experience, especially his doctrine of love.

Damascenes have kept a vivid and lively memory of the "Great Shaikh"—his tomb in al-Ṣāliḥīyah receives hundreds of visitors weekly.

* * *

According to Muslim tradition, the *'ulamā* were guardians of the law, and during the period we are considering they were very influential. *Al-waẓā'if ad-dīnīya* (religious offices) were all held by them. Thus judges, *muḥtasibs, muftīs,* teachers, imams, khatibs and qārīs were chosen from among the *'ulamā.* In such capacities they controlled education and saw to the administration of justice and the interpretation of the Law of Islam. Many of the *dīwānī* (administrative) offices were held by them, too. Khatibs of *inshā* (an office of the chancery) and nazirs of various institutions, such as *bīmāristāns* and *al-jaysh* (the army), were of the *'ulamā*. Official literature of the period certainly bears the traces of their work.

Even without holding office, many of the *'ulamā,* especially men of strong personality and character, could force their point of view on the rulers because they had the support of the public, who respected them for their learning, sincerity, and enthusiasm. A few examples will suffice to illustrate this. Al-Ādil (the Ayyūbid) issued new coins, which were called *qarāṭīs*. Al-Yūnīnī criticized this action in strong words and accused the former of intending to corrupt business transactions. On hearing this, al-Ādil canceled the *qarāṭīs*. Sibṭ ibn al-Jawzī acted as an unofficial counselor to al-Mu'aẓẓam. Al-Ẓāhir Baybars held a special council of the *'ulamā* in Damascus in 1267, to secure from them a *fatwa* for the confiscation of the lands of al-Ghūṭah, but he was faced with the opposition of Shahrazūrī, who objected to the issue of such a *fatwa* on the grounds that the sultan had no legal right to the land. The sultan succumbed to their decision. Ibn 'Abd al-Salām, himself a contemporary of al-Ẓāhir, forced the abolition of the sale of wine, struck the *bī'a* (acclamation) to the caliph before the sultan himself, and insisted that he (Ibn 'Abd al-Salām) should sell the Mamlūk amirs—and did so. He spent the proceeds in acts of charity. In 1281 wines and prostitutes were distributed by favor in Damascus, but all of this was abolished because of the opposition of the *'ulamā* and the pious.

Ibn Taymīyah is a good example of the influence of a strong *'ālim* in the affairs of state and of society. A few examples, taken from his life, reveal this. He talked to people about *jihād* (holy war) when he saw the Mongol danger in 1298, and his pleading was more effective than the orders of the sultan. When the Ghāzān's Mongols occupied Damascus, it was Ibn Taymīyah who told Arghwāsh, *nāyib al-qal'a,* not to surrender the citadel. Ibn Taymīyah, accompanied by some notables of Damascus, went to al-Nabk, hoping to meet Ghāzān in person and secure from him some sort of *amān* (amnesty) for the people of the city, but he failed to see him. After the withdrawal of Ghāzān's army from Damascus, Ibn Taymīyah and his friends visited wine shops, breaking wine vessels, pouring out their contents, and administering *ta'zīr* (admonition) to owners of *ḥānāt* (drinking places). Ibn Taymīyah accompanied the two expeditions to Kisrawān early in the fourteenth century. Before the Battle of Shaqḥab (1302), he went with the army, spoke to the men about unity and victory, saw that the amirs and other people swore to be faithful, and took the trouble to explain the legality of fighting the Mongols, although the latter were Muslims like the Syrians themselves.

I have given these few examples to illustrate the part which the *'ulamā* played in public life. If we add to this their intellectual activities, we should not be surprised to find that they had so much voice in guiding people and directing their various affairs.

Damascus literally swarmed with *'ulamā* during the Mamlūk era. They had migrated from Jazira, Baghdad, and Palestine, and in Damascus they received encouragement, security, and the opportunity of developing their interests.

A strong trend in Damascus during the fourteenth century was an intense interest in *ḥadīths*. A large number of *mu-*

ḥaddithīn made it their duty to ascertain, classify, and categorize the *ḥadīths* of Muḥammad, especially since by that time hundreds of sayings had come to be erroneously, either by accident or design, ascribed to the Prophet. The science of *ḥadīth* found its renaissance in Damascus at the hands of some of the most eminent people that science ever knew in Islam—such men as al-Muwaffaq, al-Nawawī, al-Dhahabī, al-Subkī, Ibn al-Taqī, and others.

The science of *ḥadīth* was never separated from other branches of legal studies, so one should not be surprised to find the same person excelling in both *ḥadith* and *fiqh* (jurisprudence). However, one thing should be borne in mind in this connection, namely, that the science of *ḥadīth* was always the same, irrespective of the rite or school of law to which a person belonged, while *fiqh* differed according to the rite. This is why *ḥadīth* schools, in Damascus or anywhere else, were common to all but it was not so with schools of *fiqh,* which were Shāfi'ite, Ḥanafite, Malikite, or Ḥanbalite.

The Ḥanbalites were markedly strong and influential in Damascus during the thirteenth, fourteenth, and fifteenth centuries. Two migrations, mentioned above, contributed to this: the followers of the Palestinian Ibn Qudāma left their homes near Nablus and settled in Damascus, and the Taymīyah family moved to the city from Ḥarrān (in northeast Syria). The Banu Qudāma, as they were called, produced numerous scholars, whose major contribution to their profession was the collection of *fiqh* and the preparation of encyclopedic legal works. The Taymīyah family gave Damascus Ibn Taymīyah (d. 1328), who was probably the greatest *fiqh* scholar of his time. He represents, so to speak, the "second rank," after the four

Sunnite imams, whose lot it was to revitalize Muslim legal thinking, reclassify many of Islam's earlier views, and to apply the new logic to problems unknown to earlier jurists. It is scarcely correct to speak of Ibn Taymīyah and his followers as reformers in the strict sense of the word, but their imprint, and especially Ibn Taymīyah's own, is noticeable in Muslim revivalists down to the present time.

History seems to have been an attractive proposition to many people, and they produced first-class studies. Generally speaking, earlier Muslim chroniclers were, shall we say, "closed" historians to whom only Islam and its development were valuable. They hardly worried about earlier and even contemporary non-Muslim nations. The historians of Mamlūk times, on the other hand, were "open." They wrote about Islam and Muslim peoples and countries, but after all, they had already had more contact, deeper relations, and wider dealings with peoples from the East and West: they came after many, many geographers and travelers had studied the world and had written about it. They could not, therefore, even if they wanted to do so, ignore other nations. In addition, some of them set down in writing the history of the greatest conflict Islam had with Christianity—the Crusades. Never mind what attitudes they took, what is important is that they dealt with the subject. Their horizons were, by force of circumstances, wider. I hold the view that it is to those historians of the fourteenth century that we owe the task of writing history in Arabic; they were the forerunners of Ibn Khaldūn. Damascus and its historians played a great role in all this.

The centuries we are considering were also a period of encyclopedic works in various branches of learning. This applies to *fiqh,* as al-Muwaffaq's *al-Mughnī* attests; to history, as the works of Ibn al-Athir, Ibn Kathīr, Ibn al-Furāt, and al-Dhahabī show; and to the encyclopedic works per se, as that of al-'Umari, *Masālik al-abṣār,* proves. This last work, to which reference will be made again later, is a compendium, in twenty-one volumes, of the geography, history, politics, and literature of the age. It was, in its time, also a detailed official handbook for people in government offices.

It would be useful, for wider appreciation of the various aspects of intellectual life in Damascus during the period under consideration, to place before the reader short biographical sketches of a few of the great *'ulamā* and *faqīhs,* for this will make it possible for him to have a better acquaintance with the whole atmosphere. I have endeavored to select a few whose lives and achievements will serve the purpose.

Al-Muwaffaq was ten years old when his family, of the Banu Qudāma, migrated from Palestine and settled in Damascus. The child was exposed to the acquired knowledge of his father and other prominent *'ulamā* in Damascus. Later he pursued his education at Baghdad, which he visited several times, at Mosul, and at Mecca. He was about thirty when he finally settled in Damascus and occupied himself with teaching and writing until his death in 1223. His classes were attended by numerous students, some advanced in the echelons of learning. He was principally a *faqīh,* and a Ḥanbalite, and his singular contribution to Islamic legal studies in a ten-volume encyclopedic work called *al-Mughnī,* which is a landmark in *fiqh* books because of its frequent comparative nature, so that students can easily find in it numerous legal and theological Ḥanbalite views compared with those of other Sunnite rites. It has been said about al-Muwaffaq that he was almost a *mujtahid,* that is, a man who managed to find new interpretations to certain facets of the Sharia.

Ibn Taymīyah, the jurist par excellence of the period, will be discussed more fully later. At present, I would like to mention a few other people who come from other fields of learning. One such person is al-Dhahabī (d.1348), the historian whose work *Tārīkh al-Islam* (*History of Islam*) was in seventy parts, each dealing with ten years. His knowledge was immense and his acquaintance with sources enormous, so that his work is encyclopedic in nature. His successor in the field of history is Ibn Kathīr, who wrote *al-Bidāya wal-nihāya,* in fourteen volumes. Both men epitomized earlier works for the first centuries of Islam, but they, like many others of that period, seem to have been conscious of writing the story of stirring times and thus settled down to their work seriously, leaving a wealth of detail which has been more than beneficial to us. Ibn Kathīr, especially, presents so many vivid pictures of the events and happenings of his day that we can follow them day by day.

The Damascene encyclopedist of the age is al-'Umari (d. 1348), author of *Masālik al-abṣār fī mamālik al-amṣār.* Both his father and his grandfather were in the service of the Mamlūks and held high administrative posts; they were especially connected with the organization of *al-barīd*. Al-'Umari was born in Damascus, where he obtained his early education in Arabic, jurisprudence, and ḥadīth and at one time held the office of judge. Eventually, he followed in the footsteps of his father and grandfather and joined *diwān al-inshā* (the chancery). This gave him his spur to write his voluminous *al-*

Masālik. The work is partly a book of geography dealing with the earth at large, but when he discussed political geography, he confined himself to the lands of Islam (hoping that he would discuss the lands of the infidels on another occasion). However, this is not a fair description of the book, for one finds in it a great deal of contemporaneous historical material, as well as matters concerning administration and relations between the sultan and his governors and officials. Questions of taxes, revenues, feudal rewards, and usufruct are fully discussed. The descriptions he gives of various towns, especially those of the immediate area, are accurate and full. His style represents that of the period, but he would not sacrifice accuracy to flowery writing. The book also contains, although by no means the only work of the period which does so, many royal decrees and injunctions issued on various occasions. An understanding of the Mamlūk administration cannot be complete without a thorough acquaintance with *al-Masālik*.

Ibn Ṭūlūn was born too late under the Mamlūks to enjoy their patronage in full, for he died in 1546, nearly three decades after their empire had collapsed. He is, all the same, a product of their period, for he was born forty-two years before the Ottomans entered Damascus (1516).

Ibn Ṭūlūn produced nothing original, but he was a genuine learned man of the period. His education covered Koranic sciences, *fiqh,* ḥadīth, Sufism (rather unusual, except, probably, for its refutation), language, history, mathematics, astronomy, engineering, and medicine, and his writings, more than seven hundred tomes, covered as many fields. He is a typical *'ālim* of the period—intelligent enough to learn everything he comes across, capable of digesting that knowledge, and equally capable of reproducing it in a presentable form; however, the problems of the age do not seem to have stirred him to any special consideration of them. But, in all fairness to Ibn Ṭūlūn, he was not the only man of that time who did not concern himself with more than learning and teaching in the traditional way.

The man who rose to the level of the problems of his time and tried to deal with them with knowledge, frankness, and intelligent approach was Ibn Taymīyah (1263–1328). Not only are his works interesting, but his life was exemplary. Nothing daunted him once he was convinced that he was right. That is why I propose to deal with his life a little more fully.

Aḥmad Ibn Taymīyah was seven years old when his family migrated from Ḥarrān (the Carhae of the Ancients) to Damascus. They left in fear of more Mongol invasions. Damascus had become, in the twelfth century, a center of Ḥanbalite learning, a position which was enhanced after 1258, when the Mongols destroyed Baghdad. Since his family was Ḥanbalite, Aḥmad had a unique opportunity of being exposed, from the very beginning, to the best Ḥanbalite teachers and learning of the age. The Ḥanbalite schools had produced great jurisconsults, *mutakallimīn* (theologians, scholastics), and commentators and exigesists. Their *'ulamā* paid special attention to sermons at mosques, *madrasahs,* and *zāwiyas,* and Ibn Taymīyah had excellent opportunities to be part and parcel of all this. At the age of twenty-two, he succeeded his father, who had died the previous year, as teacher, a sign of recognition of his knowledge. His lessons seem to have had wide reputation, not only for followers of other Sunnite rites, but also for some Shī'ites who attended his classes.

The age in which Ibn Taymīyah lived was dominated by Ash'arism, permeated with Sufism, and readily accepted traditional attitudes. Ibn Taymīyah was hostile to all these, and from the beginning he waged an unremitting war against them. This is what eventually won for him the name of "reformer."

Ibn Taymīyah took an active part in the life of his city and his community. His "harshness" against his opponents produced violent reactions, hence they accused him of being intransigent and demanded from the authorities that he be punished. So the man spent a few years in prison in Cairo and Damascus. His last days were spent at the citadel of Damascus, where he died.

Ibn Taymīyah was not only an *'ālim* who taught and wrote; he was, like numerous Ḥanbalites throughout history, an activist. He voluntarily took it upon himself to see that people, high before low, behaved themselves according to the best Muslim tradition. This was the duty of *al-muhṭasib,* but Ibn Taymīyah was an active and dynamic (although self-appointed) *muhṭasib* himself.

Ibn Taymīyah has left numerous works dealing with many matters. I have no intention of discussing his books here, but I would like to place before the reader a few of his more important views and attitudes.

He discussed, in *al-Wāsiṭīya* and in other works, the Muslim *'aqīda* (credo), which, as he saw, had suffered as a result of Ash'arism, Sufism, and traditionalism. Some Muslims had come to accept the view that God had bodily attributes *(ṣifāt),* basing these conclusions on allegoric interpretations of certain verses in the Qur'ān. Ibn Taymīyah returned to—and expected every Muslim to return to—the Holy Book and the Sunna of the Prophet for a sound, thorough, correct, and genuine understanding of the *'aqīda,* discarding all methods and ideas of interpretation that had come from outside Islam, such as allegory, anthropomorphism, and *tashbīh* (comparison between the world of God and the physical world).

Neither could Ibn Taymīyah accept the two extreme views of the Sufis—*ḥulūl* (incarnation) and *ittiḥād* (mystic union). To him, such things were of the nature of *shirk,* which Islam could not accept, hence his unrelenting attacks on Ibn 'Arabi, although Ibn Taymīyah did not attack Sufis or Sufism generally. Sufis, however, took advantage of his stand, accused him before the sultan in Cairo, and managed to have him imprisoned, but then Ibn Taymīyah had created such antangonism that his enemies were legion.

The traditionalists suffered greatly at the hands of Ibn Taymīyah. According to a custom by then some five centuries old, jurists were compelled when discussing problems of law, to do so within the area of the four Sunnite rites or schools; in other words, they could not follow their own individual interpretations. This is known in Islam as the closing of *bāb al-ijtihād* (the door of personal interpretation). Ḥanbalites had not, strictly speaking, adhered to this, but they must have succumbed to tradition in some areas. Ibn Taymīyah held that *ijtihād* was an essential and continuous process for the Muslim society. This intellectual attitude was explained through many *fatwas,* or legal opinions, in which Ibn Taymiyah showed originality of approach without seeking any bases for his arguments outside the Qur'ān and the Ḥadīth, strengthened by the *ijmā'* (concensus of opinion) of the Prophet's companions.

The bases which jurists used in their legal interpretations were *ijmā', qiyas* (analogy), and sometimes *ra'y* (opinion), Ibn Taymīyah challenged these, concluding that the *ijmā'* of the *'ulamā* could be reconsidered, which meant that views of the four masters of the Sunnite rites were subject to rethinking whenever an opportunity, with the Qur'ān or the Ḥadīth as guides, presented itself.

It is interesting to note that Ibn Taymīyah was not alone in this field. Ibn 'Abd al-Salām and Ibn al-Qayyim did not avow the blind acceptance of the verdicts of the four imams. The former did not want the public to be allowed a free *ijtihād*. The latter thought that *fiqh* was a growing and evolutionary process to provide the means adopted by the state for the *maslaḥa* (welfare) of the community.

* * *

Ibn Taymīyah figured prominently in many other problems which Damascene *'ulamā* considered. A few of the issues they discussed will reveal the nature of their activity and dynamism.

THE CULT OF THE HOLY LAND

One of the most interesting aspects of religious discussions in the Mamlūk period was the interest people took in the Holy Land. Three books written during this era show how deeply the matter was rooted in the minds of the *'ulamā: Targhīb ahl al-Islām fī sukna al-Shām,* by 'Izz ad-Dīn Ibn 'Abd al-Salām (known as Sulṭān al'Ulamā); *Muthīr al-Gharām fī ziyārat al-Quds wal-Shām,* by Shihāb ad-Dīn al-Maqdisī; and *Muthīr al-Gharām fī ziyārat al-Khalīl'ām,* by al-Tadmuri al-Khalīlī.

The thesis developed in the first book, seemingly representative of many others, was that according to many traditions of the Prophet, al-Shām (Syria) as a whole—Damascus in particular—was especially sacred to Muslims. Many companions of the Prophet were buried in Syria, and the country was therefore vital to Islam and should thus be defended by Muslims. The first *Muthīr* emphasized Jerusalem, while the second stressed Hebron.

The Cult of the Holy Land had become so strong in the thirteenth century that Ibn Taymīyah found it expedient and useful to refute such an argument, which, from his iconoclastic point of view, was outrageous. So he wrote his *Qā'ida fī ziyārat bayt al-Maqdis*. His refutations may be summed up as follows: (1) Al-Masjid (the Mosque of Jerusalem) was the third mosque in importance, but that of al-Khalīl, in Hebron, did not rank as equal. (2) The Masjid of Jerusalem served as a place of worship of God, like any other mosque, but a visit to it did not take the place of the pilgrimage to Mecca. (3) There was no *ḥaram* (sanctuary) attached to either Jerusalem or Hebron, as was the case with Mecca. (4) A visit to the Masjid of Jerusalem was an ordinary matter and was permissable at any time, but it could never be considered as a pilgrimage. (5) 'Asqalān, 'Akkā, and Ṭarsūs (Anṭarsūs) might not be visited (i.e., with a religious purpose) because they had been destroyed.

Ibn Taymīyah, *inter alia,* tried to show that many of the

traditions accepted as authentic by many people were far from being so and that they were the creation of later *quṣṣāṣ* (storytellers).

MAN'S RELATION TO GOD

One of the burning questions of the period concerned man's relation to God. There were at least two lines of argument on this point. First, there was the Sufi interpretation which seems to have attracted a large number of followers and which, through the organization of Sufism in *ṭarīqahs,* drew more and more attention from the *'ulamā*. The second line of thought was the Sunnite, taught in the traditional Ash'-arite school and the newly developed Ḥanbalite school, which had been growing rapidly between the twelfth and fourteenth centuries.

At various stages and after various thinkers, Sufism taught *ḥulūl* and *ittiḥād,* to which was added, in the thirteenth century, *waḥdat al-wujūd* (existentialist monism). Sufis insisted that *ma'rifa* was the means by which man could know God. Many of them, if not all, were prepared to admit foreign practices or to neglect some forms of worship; thus Sufi *ṭarīqahs* admitted *dhikr* and *samā'* as means of gaining *ma'rifa.* We have seen that the leading Sufi of the period was Ibn 'Arabi. When Ibn Taymīyah refuted Sufism, he naturally chose Ibn 'Arabi as his target.

Sunnism, on the other hand, maintained high moral and intellectual standards and refused to countenance innovations and usages which detracted from the purity of early doctrines. And in its refutation of Sufism, as well as in its re-examination and explanation of Islam, Sunnism was vigorous. Ibn Taymīyah, as has been said, was probably the strongest leader of Sunnite (Ḥanbalite) thought of the period.

A Muslim—and that was a central problem to Ibn Taymīyah and his contemporaries, for Islam was the only religion acceptable to God—was expected to believe in God and His Prophet. A Muslim drew on the Qur'ān and the Sunna for his belief because all matters of faith and action were fully treated there. The *īmān* (belief) of a Muslim, which would guarantee salvation, was "a belief in God alone, which is the basis of religion, and accepting Muḥammad as His Prophet." The emphasis of Ibn Taymīyah that faith was a unit, that is, indivisible, is interesting. This certainly included worship as prescribed in the two sources of Islam. In addition, man must submit to God, and his submission, like his faith, should be complete.

God revealed himself to man through the prophets, Muḥammad being the last messenger of God. Man might, when asking God's help, seek the intercession of the Prophet, but Ibn Taymīyah took exception to visiting sanctuaries and tombs of *walīs* (saints) in the belief that such places and men enjoyed special powers, bestowed special blessings, and acted as intermediaries between man and his creator. He thus strongly denounced such visits and took a great deal of trouble to point out that God never favored such tombs with any special place or power.

MAN AND THE COMMUNITY

Al-umma (the community), as Ibn Taymīyah conceived of it, was the community of Muslims. The basic principle according to which members of the community worked together was *ta'āwun* (solidarity), where each Muslim was to see that other men were helped to do good, avoid evil, and receive justice according to the principles of Islam. Furthermore, Ibn Taymīyah thought of the community as organic and having definite aims and ends. The purpose of the community was *al-amr bil-ma'ruf wal-nahy 'an al-munkar* (to commend goodness and condemn evil-doing). Here again, the community was fulfilling the will of God.

In order that the community may achieve its end, it must have an organization, an *imāma,* or state, which, with its various administrative officers and bodies, should comply with the teachings of Islam. It should aim at *al-amr bilma'ruf wal-nahy 'an al-munkar;* it should be a just state, for God may not help an unjust state, although the latter may be a state of believers. The state which Ibn Taymīyah advocated was theocratic, but, as Henri Laoust has suggested, its duty was to co-operate with and serve the *umma* and not merely to receive the latter's submission. Subordinance, however, was essential for the achievement of the end for which a community existed. The state had an ethical duty toward the community, both in social and economic life. It should secure justice, attend to security, and see that people performed their religious practices. Through *al-muḥtasib* it should see that all kinds of transactions were just and should protect the population against fraud.

The duty of the state in economic life included the protection of the community against monopolies and fraudulent merchants. Control of prices was permitted only when it would help people to maintain their rights—in times of shortage and need. Ibn Taymīyah allowed the state to interfere in the economic affairs of the community only for securing its needs. Thus individuals could be directed to perform certain duties in trades, agriculture, or war when the interest of the community demanded it, but such duties were to be compensated, and no one was to suffer injustice.

Ibn Taymīyah was not in favor of individual economy. The individual was not the undisputed master of his actions: his initiative was subject to the injunctions of Islam. It was the duty of the state to see that such rules were observed.

THE *Jihād* (HOLY WAR)

The empire of the Mamlūks came into existence while the Crusaders were still in the area, and the latter had to be fought until they were expelled. But the danger of further attempts by Europeans to invade the area was ever present, and there were several abortive attempts at Alexandria and Nicopolis, to mention only two cases. Some elements of the population were accused of assisting the Europeans. From the state's point of view, they were traitors and could be punished, either individually or collectively.

The Mongols invaded Syria and her neighbors many times, and campaigns were waged against them with various degrees of success or failure. They, too, had sympathizers among the native population. Were these people also traitors? If so, on what grounds?

All of these matters pertaining to the wars of the period were discussed. The Europeans were Christians, so the Muslim state was not only free to wage war against them but was duty bound, through the sultan, to wage a *jihād* (holy war). But the Mongols had been converted. Was it legal to fight against them? We have seen that Ibn Taymīyah led the fight against them in person, and if he had not been convinced of the correctness of his attitude, he would certainly never have taken such a step. His view on the subject was quite clear. The Mongols were Muslims, but their behavior and their atrocities against Muslims in Iraqi and North Syrian towns and villages placed them in the same category as common criminals; therefore, they should be fought. Their sympathizers were mainly Shī'ites, and Ibn Taymīyah certainly had no love for these people. He therefore accompanied a group of soldiers who attacked the Shī'ite strongholds in the Syrian and Lebanese mountains.

* * *

The '*ulamā* of the Mamlūk period left an imprint not only on their own age but on posterity as well. In this, the name of Ibn Taymīyah stands foremost as the reformer of the period, mainly because of his dynamism, clarity of thought, easy style (for a *faqih* and legalist), and his frankness. Many were the followers of Ibn Taymīyah, and one of the most prominent was Ibn al-Qayyim (al-Jawziyīa, d.1350). Of those non-Ḥanbalites who were greatly influenced by Ibn Taymīyah's views, I mention al-Dhahabī, Ibn Kathīr, and Ibn Ḥajar, three prominent historians and '*ulamā* of the period, as being outstanding. Ibn Taymīyah's influence in Egypt was enormous during his lifetime.

It is interesting to note that some '*ulamā* of Baghdad, the capital which had been destroyed by Hūlāgu seventy years earlier, upon hearing that Ibn Taymīyah was to be imprisoned in the citadel of Damascus, wrote to Sultan al-Nāṣir pleading the case of Shaikh al-Islām. The letter reads in part:

> When it became known to the people of the Eastern countries and Iraqi provinces that Shaikh al-Islām, Taqiy al-Dīn Aḥmad Ibn Taymīyah, may God grant him health, was being subjected to confinement, Muslims were greatly distressed, and men of religion [Islam] became sad. . . . When the 'Ulamā of this region realized the magnitude of the tragedy . . . they wrote to the Sultan . . . supporting the Shaikh in his fatwas, mentioning his learning and virtues, and addressed this to the Sultan . . . in defense of his religion and for rendering an advice to the princes of the faithful in favour of Islam.

The conquest of Syria by the Ottomans weakened the position of the Ḥanbalites and Ḥanbalite learning because the conquerors were Ḥanafites. For a long time Ibn Taymīyah was practically forgotten in his own country and city. Probably the Sufis, who were rather favored by the Ottomans (Selim, on capturing Damascus, had a *zāwiya* built on the tomb of Ibn 'Arabi), were partly responsible for this. It was in foreign lands, however, that Ibn Taymīyah came to be known, studied, and followed. In the middle of the eighteenth century, Muḥammad ibn 'Abdul Wahhāb preached his revivalist call in Najd along the same lines of thought as those of Ibn Taymīyah. Almost a century later, Muḥammad ibn Ali al-Sanūsī, founded his reform movement in Libya; Ibn Taymīyah's influence is discernible in many of his teachings. Early in the present century, Rashid Riḍā, the publisher-editor of *al-Manār* and a leading Salafī, proclaimed himself an heir of Ibn Taymīyah.

Ibn Taymīyah, then, set the pattern for Islamic reform and revivalism. It has been followed by revivalists and reformers ever since.

Bibliography

PRIMARY SOURCES

'Arabī, Muhiyiddīn Ibn. *Tarjuman al-ashwaq*. London, 1911.

'Asākir, 'Ali ibn al-Hasan Ibn. *Tārīkh madinat Dimashq*. Ed. by Ṣalāhuddīn al-Munajjid. Damascus, 1945. Vol. II, Part I.

Badri, 'Abdullah al-. *Nuzhat al-ānām fī maḥāsin al-Shām*. Cairo, 1341 A.H.

Baṭṭū ṭah, Muḥammad ibn 'Abdullah Ibn. *Tuḥfat al-nuẓẓār fī 'ajāyib al-asfār*. Tr. by Sir Hamilton Gibb. Cambridge, 1958. Vol. I.

Benjamin of Tudela. *The Travels of Rabbi Benjamin*. In *Early Travels in Palestine*. Ed. by Th. Wright. London, 1848.

Brocquiere, Bertrandon de la. *The Travels of Bertrandon de la Brocquiere*. In *Early Travels in Palestine*. Ed. by Th. Wright. London, 1848.

Fida, Ismā'il ibn 'Ali Abū al-. *Al-mukhtaṣar fī akhbār al-bashar*. Istanbul, 1268 A.H.

———. *Taqwīm al-buldān*. Ed. by Reinaud and De Slane. Paris, 1840.

Frescobaldi, Lionardo, Giorgio Gucci, and Simone Sigoli. *Visit to the Holy Places of Egypt, Sinai, Palestine and Syria in A.D.*

1384. Ed. by Theophilus Bellorini and Eugene Hoade. Jerusalem, 1948.

Furāt, Muḥammad Ibn al-. *Tārīkh*. Ed. by Constantine K. Zurayk and Nalja Izzadīn. Beirut, 1936–38. Vols. VIII and IX.

Jama'a, Muḥammad ibn Abu-Bakr Ibn. *Taḥrīr al-aḥkām*. Ed. by Hans Kofler. In *Islamaica,* Vol. VI (1934) and Vol. VII (1935).

Jubayr, Muḥammad ibn Aḥmad Ibn. *Rihla*. Tr. by R. J. C. Broadhurst. London, 1952.

Kathīr, Ismā'il ibn 'Umar Ibn. *Al-bidāya wal-nihāya*. Cairo. 1358 A.H. Vol. XIV.

Niccolo of Poggobonsi. *A Voyage Beyond the Seas*. Tr. from the Italian by Theophilus Bellorini and Eugene Hoade. Jerusalem, 1945.

Qalqashandī, Shihāb al-Din al-. *Ṣubḥ al-a'shā*. 14 vols. Cairo, 1913–19.

Qudāma, Muwaffaq al-Dīn Ibn. *Al-mughnī*. 12 vols. Cairo, 1346–48 A.H.

Shāma, 'Abdul-Raḥmān al-. *Dhayl kitāb ar-rawḍatayn*. Published under the title *Tarājim rijāl al-qarnayn al-sādis was-sābi'*. Cairo. 1366/1947.

Shayzarī, 'Abdul-Raḥmān al-. *Nihāyat al-rutba fī ṭalab al-ḥisba*. Ed. by Sayyid al-'Arini. Cairo, 1946.

Taghri-Birdi, Yūsuf Ibn. *An-nujūm az-zāhira fī akhbār Misr wal-Qāhira*. Ed. by William Popper. 6 vols. Berkeley, 1908–29.

Taymīyah, Taqiy al-Dīn Ibn. *Kitāb al-siyāsa al-shar'iye*. Cairo, 1316 A.H.

———. *Bughyat al-murtād*. Cairo, 1323 A.H.

———. *Al-ḥisba fil-islām*. In *Majmu'at rasā'il*. Cairo, 1323 A.H.

———. *Majmu'at al-rasā'il al-kubra*. 2 vols. Cairo, 1323 A.H.

———. *Fatāwa*. 5 vols. Cairo, 1325–29 A.H.

———. *Rasā'il wa-masā'il*. Ed. by al-Manar. 3 vols. Cairo, 1346 A.H.

———. *Qā'ida fī ziyārat bayt al-Maqdis*. Ed. by Charles D. Mathews. In *Journal of the American Oriental Society*. Vol. LVI (1936).

Ṭulun, Muḥammad ibn 'Ali Ibn. *Tārīkh al-Ṣāliḥīya*. Ed. by Muḥammad A. Dahmān. 2 vols. Damascus, 1949.

'Umarī, Ibn Fadl al-Allah al-. *Masālik al-abṣār fī mamālik al-amṣār*. MS, Oxford, Pocock, 191.

Ẓāhirī, Khalīl al-. *Ẓubdat kashf al-Mamālik*. Ed. by Ravisso. Paris, 1891.

Zettersteen, K. V. *Tārīkh salāṭīn al-Mamālīk*. Leiden, 1919.

MODERN STUDIES

Afiifi, A. E. *The Mystical Philosophy of Muhyid Din Ibnul 'Arabi*. Cambridge, 1939.

Arberry, Arthur J. *Sufism*. London, 1950.

Ecochard, Michel, and Claude Le Coeur. *Les Baines de Damas*. Beirut, 1940.

Gaudefroy-Demombyne, Maurice. *La Syrie à l'époque des Mamlouks d'àprés les Auteurs Arabes*. Paris, 1923.

Gibb, Sir Hamilton. *Arabic Literature*. 2nd ed. Oxford, 1963.

Laoust, Henri. *Essai sur les Doctrines Sociales et Politiques de Taki-Din Ahmad B. Taymiyya*. Cairo, 1939.

Sauvaget, Jean. *Esquisse d'une Histoire de la Ville de Damas*. In *Revue Études Islamiques,* 1934.

Smith, Margaret. *Readings from the Mystics of Islam*. London, 1950.

Terresse, René. *L'Irrigation dans la Ghouta de Damas*. In *Revue Études Islamiques,* 1929.

Ziadeh, Nicola A. *Urban Life in Syria under the Early Mamlūks*. Beirut, 1953.

Index

'Abbāsids: 4, 97
'Abd al-Qādir al-Jilānī: 94
'Abd al-Salām, 'Izz ad-Dīn Ibn: 113, 123
'Abdul Hādī, Ibn: 54
Abu'l Rabī' Sulayman ibn Ibrāhīm ibn Mālik: 67
Abū Shāma: 92, 100
Abū 'Umar Ibn Qudāma al-Maqdisī (the Jerusalemite): 49–50, 54, 115
Acre: 80–81
Ādil, al- (the Ayyūbid): 35, 113
'Adilīya Court: 80
Ahadith: *see* Ḥadīth
Akhḍar, al-: 38
'Akkā: 124
Aleppo: xiv, 16, 52, 79f., 92, 97
Alexandria: 128
'Ali al-Dakhwār, Ibn: 57
Almohades: 102
Amana River: 25
Amat al-Laṭīf: 73
'Arabi, Ibn: 97, 101–12, 122, 125
Aramaeans: xv
Arghwāsh: 7f., 114
Armenia: 13, 35
Ash'arism: 93, 121, 125
Ashraf Khalīl, al-: 5, 36
'Asqalān: 124
Athir, Ibn al-: 117
Ayyūbids: 4, 20, 34f., 52, 79, 89, 92, 97, 100

Bāb al-Barīd (Gate of the Postal Service): 27, 55
Bāb al-Faraj (Gate of Consolation): 8, 20
Bāb al-Jābiya: 25
Bāb al-Shāmīya: 80
Bāb Jairūn: 27
Bāb Sharqi: 25

Bāb Tūma (St. Thomas Gate): 60
Badr al-Dīn: 83
Badri, al-: 38
Baghdad: xiv, 5, 52, 92, 94, 97, 102, 114, 117, 120, 129
Banu al-Sūfī: 19
Banu Qudāma: 97, 115, 117
Barsbāy: 16
Battle of ʻAyn Jālūt: 6
Battle of Ḥiṭṭīn: 3, 92
Battle of Shaqḥab: 114
Batuta, Ibn: 40–41, 48, 50, 64, 69
Baybars, al-Ẓāhir: 4f., 36, 38, 52, 79, 93, 113
Bayn al-Nahrayn: 22, 51
Beirut: xiv, 63
Benjamin of Tudela: 25, 60
Bīmāristān al-Qaymarī: 55–56

Cairo: 15, 52, 79, 97, 101, 112, 121f.
Calabrians, in Damascus: 63
Catalans, in Damascus: 63
Cave of Hunger: 31
Christians: xvi, 60f., 63–64, 81, 85–87, 94
Crusaders: 5, 20, 35, 49, 92f., 100, 116, 128

Damascus: markets, xiii–xiv, 41–47, 82, 87–91; legend of, xvi–xx, 30, 61–63; government, 17–18, 52, 77–82; defense of the city, 19–20; schools, 22, 51–54; description of, 23–33; hospitals, 29, 54–57; citadel, 35–38; economic life, 34; swords, 46–47; convents, 57–59; population, 60–64; ritual in, 71–73; wealth and earnings in, 73–75; monetary system, 88; literature, 98–112
Dār al-Biṭṭīkh wal-Fakiha (Market of Melons and Fruits): 82
Dāwūd, Ibn: 59
Dhahabī, al-: 115, 117f., 129
Dirʻa: xiv
Ḍiyāʼīya, al-: 54

East Gate: 60

Fāriḍ, Ibn al-: 97
Fatimids: 92
Feast of Shaʻbān: 53
Florentines, in Damascus: 63
Frederick II: 3
Frenchmen, in Damascus: 63
Frescobaldi, Lionardo: 42
Furāt, Ibn al-: 117

Genoese, in Damascus: 63
Ghawri, al-: 13, 15
Ghazālī, al-: 95–96
Ghāzān: 6–8, 11, 36, 73, 81, 114
Ghūṭah: xiii–xiv, xviii, 22, 24, 51, 113

Great Umayyad Mosque: xvi, 25–29, 40–41, 71, 84
Greeks: 94
Green Palace of Mu'āwiyah: xv
Grotto of Adam: 31
Gucci, Giorgio: 36, 42

Hadīth: 41, 94, 123
Ḥajar, Ibn: 129
Hall of Justice: 38, 72
Ḥamīdīyah: xv
Ḥanafism: 52, 79, 115
Ḥanbal, Aḥmad Ibn: 50
Ḥanbalism: 50, 52, 54, 79, 115, 117, 120–22, 125, 130
Ḥarrān (Carhae): 115, 120
Haṣa, al-: 38
Hebron: 124
Ḥijāz: xiv, 35
Ḥimṣ: 6
Ḥiṭṭīn: 3, 92
Hūlāgu: 130

Ibrāhīm al-Ḥalabī: 14
Indians: 94
Ishmaelites: 84, 91

Jabal al-Aḥmar: 14
Jabal Qāsyūn: *see* Qāsyūn
Jabha, al-: 51
Jābiya Gate: 60
Jacobites: 85
Jalāl al-Dīn al-Rumi: 94
Jamāl al-Miṣrī, al-: 80
Jazira: 114
Jenin: 16
Jerusalem: 16, 49, 124
Jews: xvi, 60, 63–64, 86–87
Jabayr, Ibn: 20, 23–33, 38–39, 58, 61, 64
Juwānīya, al-: 53

Kamāl, al-: 73
Kāmil, al-: 3
Karak, al-: 16
Kathīr, Ibn: 6, 117f., 129
Khaldūn, Ibn: 97, 116
Khalīl, al-: 124
Khidr, al- (Elijah): 32, 49
Khizāna, al-: 80
Khushqadam: 14
Kisrawān: 114
Kiswah, al-: 10
Koran: *see* Qur'ān
Kurds: 60

La Brocquiere, Bertrandon de: 37, 39, 42, 46–47, 64
Lebanon: 5, 13, 92

Maghrib: 28, 38, 67f.
Malikites: 28, 52, 79, 115
Maqdisī, Shihāb ad-Dīn al-: 124
Marj Dābiq: 15
Maronites: 13
Masjid, al-: 124
Mawlawīya, al-: 94
Mayāfārqīn: 101
Maydān al-Akhḍar: 36
Maydān al-Khayl: 72

Maydān Taḥt al-Qal'a (Citadel Square): 21, 31, 34, 38, 72
Mecca: 117, 124
Melchites: 85
Mesopotamia: xiv
Mizzah, al-: 7, 33, 48, 72
Mongols: 5–13, 35, 97, 114, 120, 128–29
Mosque of Abū Ṣāliḥ: 50
Mosque of Jerusalem: *see* Masjid, al-
Mosul: 3, 117
Mount Qāsyūn: *see* Qāsyūn
Mu'aẓẓam, al-: 113
Muḥummad (the Prophet of Islam): xix, 39, 126
Muḥammad ibn 'Abdul Wahhāb: 130
Muḥammad ibn Ali al-Sanūsī: 130
Munajjā, Ibn: 50
Murcia (Andalusia): 102
Muwaffaq, al-: 73
Muẓaffar, al-: 73

Nabk, al-: 114
Nablus: 16, 86, 115
Nāṣir Muḥammad, al-: 6
Nāṣir Qalāwun, al-: 5
Nawawī, al-: 115
Nayrab, al-: xix, 33, 48, 55
Niccolo of Poggibonsi: 36, 42
Nicopolis: 128
North Africa: 94
Nubāta, Ibn: 101
Nubuwīya, al-: 59
Nūr al-Dīn: 3, 29, 54, 58, 92, 99f.
Nūrī, al-: 54, 56–57
Nuṣayris: 93

Ottomans: 130

Palestine: xiv, 5f., 92, 114
Palmyra: xiv
Parpar River: 25

Qabjaq: 7f.
Qadam, al-: xix, 38
Qādirīya, al-: 58–59, 94
Qalandarīya, al-: 59
Qalqashandi, al-: 76
Qāsyūn: xviii, 31, 48ff.
Qaṭya: 51
Qayyim, Ibn al- (al-Jawziyīa): 123, 129
Qudāma, Ibn: *see* Abū 'Umar Ibn Qudāma al-Maqdisī
Qur'ān (Koran): xix, 28, 32, 40f., 49f., 63, 67f., 70, 94, 99, 122f., 126

Rabwa, al-: xix, 22, 48f.
Ramleh: 16
Riḍā, Rashid: 130
Rifā'īya, al-: 59
Rūm: *see* Christians

Sā'ātī, Ibn al-: 100

Ṣafad: 16, 81
Ṣāḥiba, al-: 54
St. Mary's Church: 61
Saladin: 3, 23–33, 35, 60, 92f., 99f.
Ṣāliḥīyah, al-: 7, 48, 50, 54f., 59, 97, 112
Saljūqs: 22, 52
Samaritans: 61, 86–87
Samarqand: 10
Saracens: 62
Sayf al-Dīn: 55
Selim I: 13, 15
Shāḍhilī, al-: 94
Shāḍhilīya, al-: 94
Shāfi'ism: 52, 79, 93, 115
Shahrazūrī: 113
Shaikh al-Islām: 130
Shām, al-: 16
Sharia: 17, 78ff., 91, 118
Shī'ism: 13, 21f., 84, 91f., 121, 129
Sibṭ ibn al-Jawzī: 113
Sidon: xiv
Sigoli, Simone: 42
Sinjir: 36
Sodon: 12
Street Called Straight: 60
Subkī, al-: 81, 115
Sufism: 30, 57ff., 70–71, 85, 93–96, 112, 119, 121f., 125, 130
Suhrawardī, al-: (al-Maqtūl): 94, 100
Suhrawardīya, al-: 94
Sultan al-Nāṣir: 11, 130
Sunnism: 21f., 54, 91ff., 95, 97, 99, 116, 118, 121, 123, 125–26
Sūq al-Kabīr (Great Market): 24
Sūq al-Khayl (Horse Market): 82
Sūq al-Raqīq (Slave Market): 82
Sūq Ṣārūja: 80

Tadmuri al-Khalīlī, al-: 124
Taghri-Birdi, Ibn: 10, 14, 16
Taḥt al-Sā'āt: 80
Taqī, Ibn al-: 115
Ṭarsus (Anṭarsūs): 124
Taymīyah, Ibn: 7–9, 96f., 113–14, 115–16, 118, 120–31
Taymīyah family: 115
Thawra: 33
Tīmūr (Tamerlane): 10–13, 36, 55f.
Tinkiz: 73
Ṭūlūn, Ibn: 119–20
Ṭūmān-bāy: 13
Turkmen: 60

'Umar, ibn: 50
'Umari, al-: 41, 76, 117f
'Umarīya, al-: 54
Umayyads: 25, 30
'Unayn, Ibn: 100

Varthema, Ludovico di: 37, 42
Venetians, in Damascus: 63
Von Suchem: 42

Wādi al-Banafsaj: 22, 51
Wādi al-Khaznadār: 7
Wafā'īya, al-: 59

Yabrūdī, al-: 83
Yalakī, al-: 22, 51
Yāqūt: 101
Yemen: 100
Yūnīnī, al-: 113

Ẓāhir, al-: *see* Baybars, al-Ẓāhir
Ẓāhirīya School: 35
Zakī, Ibn al-, Chief Justice: 102
Zangids: 20, 22, 35, 52, 60, 92, 97

DATE DUE

DE 1 4 '79

GAYLORD PRINTED IN U.S.A.